Also of Interest

African Security Issues: Sovereignty, Stability, and Solidarity, edited by Bruce E. Arlinghaus

The Challenges of South-South Cooperation, edited by Breda Pavlič, Raúl R. Uranga, Boris Cizelj, and Marjan Svetličič

Communist Nations' Military Assistance, edited by John F. Copper and Daniel S. Papp

Arab Aid to Sub-Saharan Africa, Pamela M. Mertz and Robert A. Mertz

Nigeria in Search of a Stable Civil-Military System, J. 'Bayo Adekson

The Economics of Political Instability: The Nigerian-Biafran War, E. Wayne Nafziger

†*Africa's International Relations: The Diplomacy of Dependency and Change*, Ali A. Mazrui

†*The Foreign Policy Priorities of Third World States*, edited by John J. Stremlau

†*State Versus Ethnic Claims: African Policy Dilemmas*, edited by Donald Rothchild and Victor A. Olorunsola

†*Alternative Futures for Africa*, edited by Timothy M. Shaw

†*Globalism Versus Realism: International Relations' Third Debate*, edited by Ray Maghroori and Bennett Ramberg

PROFILES OF CONTEMPORARY AFRICA:

†*Mozambique: From Colonialism to Revolution, 1900–1982*, Allen Isaacman and Barbara Isaacman

†*Tanzania: An African Experiment*, Rodger Yeager

Senegal: An African Nation Between Islam and the West, Sheldon Gellar

Botswana: Liberal Democracy and the Labor Reserve in Southern Africa, Jack Parson

†*Kenya: The Quest for Prosperity*, Norman N. Miller

†Available in hardcover and paperback.

Military Development
in Africa

Westview Special Studies on Africa

Military Development in Africa:
The Political and Economic Risks of Arms Transfers
Bruce E. Arlinghaus

Increases in the number and improvements in the quality of arms transferred to sub-Saharan African nations clearly will affect those nations' economic development and political stability both immediately and in the long term. Problems of technology absorption, manpower development, and the diversion of financial and human resources occasioned by such transfers become more and more critical as the demand for military modernization by African governments grows and the industrial nations compete to meet the demand.

Dr. Arlinghaus evaluates conflicting assessments of the costs and benefits of military development from the perspective that it would be best for African nations to allocate resources for defense on the basis of socioeconomic considerations as well as their military and political goals.

Dr. Bruce E. Arlinghaus (Major, U.S. Army) is currently a political-military affairs officer serving in the Plans Division of the Office of the Deputy Chief of Staff for Operations, Headquarters, U.S. Army, Europe. In addition to having taught anthropology and political science in the Department of Social Sciences, U.S. Military Academy, West Point (1979–1983), he has taught at Indiana University, the University of Maryland (Europe), and at the U.S. Naval Postgraduate School. He is the editor of *Arms for Africa: Military Assistance and Foreign Policy in the Developing World* and *African Security Issues: Sovereignty, Stability, and Solidarity*, and the coeditor of *Industrial Capacity and Defense Planning: Sustained Conflict and Surge Capability* (with Lee D. Olvey and Henry A. Leonard) and *African Armies: Force Modernization and Defense Policymaking in the Developing World* (with Pauline H. Baker, forthcoming).

Military Development in Africa
The Political and Economic Risks of Arms Transfers

Bruce E. Arlinghaus

Westview Press / Boulder and London

Westview Special Studies on Africa

Quotations reprinted from Theodore H. Moran, "Iranian Defense Expenditures and the Social Crisis," *International Security,* Winter 1978-1979, pp. 178–192, appear on pages 49 and 69 of this volume and are reprinted by permission of The MIT Press, Cambridge, Massachusetts.

Quotation reprinted from John D. Montgomery, *Technology and Civil Life* (Cambridge, Massachusetts: MIT Press, 1974, pp. 160–161, appear on pages 55–56 of this volume and are reprinted with permission of The MIT Press, Cambridge, Massachusetts.

Published in 1984 in the United States of America by Westview Press, Inc., 5500 Central Avenue, Boulder, Colorado 80301; Frederick A. Praeger, President and Publisher

Library of Congress Cataloging in Publication Data
Arlinghaus, Bruce E.
  Military development in Africa.
  (Westview special studies on Africa)
  Bibliography: p.
  Includes index.
  1. Africa—Military policy. 2. Munitions—Africa.
3. Africa—Politics and government—1960-
I. Title. II. Series.
UA855.A74 1984   355'.03306   83-23275
ISBN 0-86531-434-9

Printed and bound in the United States of America

10   9   8   7   6   5   4   3   2   1

In memory of
Alfred J. Berling
(1908–1976)

Thanks, Ber

Contents

Tables

Tables

Preface

Increases in the number and improvements in the quality of arms transferred to African nations clearly will affect those nations' economic development and political stability both immediately and in the long term. Problems of technology absorption, manpower development, and the diversion of financial and human resources occasioned by such transfers become more and more critical as the demand for military modernization by African governments grows and as the industrial nations compete to meet that demand. This study evaluates conflicting assessments of the costs and benefits of military development from the perspective that African nations would best allocate resources for defense on the basis of socioeconomic considerations as well as military and political goals and that such defense expenditures, even though they may be justified, may be better spent on more appropriate forms of military technology.

Research on the topic was conducted at various Department of Defense agencies and the Department of State in Washington, D.C.; at the Defense Institute for Security Assistance Management (DISAM), Wright-Patterson Air Force Base, Ohio; at the U.S. Army Institute for Military Assistance, Fort Bragg, North Carolina; and in Kenya, Brazil, and South Africa.

Support was provided by the Office of the Deputy Chief of Staff for Operations, Department of Army (for overseas travel), and the Association of Graduates, U.S. Military Academy (for conference participation and research in the United States). The royalties from this publication will be paid to the latter organization for its continuing support of West Point faculty development and research, as a small token of my appreciation for the association's assistance over the past four years.

I would be remiss if I did not acknowledge also the aid of the superintendent, dean of the academic board, and my colleagues in the Department of Social Sciences at the U.S. Military Academy. Their generous contributions of time, and especially tolerance for my absences from West Point, are greatly appreciated.

I also owe a debt to Ed Laurance and Mike Clough of the Department of National Security Affairs, U.S. Naval Postgraduate School, Monterey, California, who helped me secure a visiting professorship there in early 1982, allowing Dave Underwood, Paul Pope, John Boyer, Joe Bowab, and Mike Harbin to participate in my seminar on arms transfers to Africa, and who helped me sharpen the specifics of this analysis.

I must thank Bill Taylor of the Georgetown University Center for Strategic and International Studies for helping me become an Army Fellow there, and more importantly, while still at West Point, for inspiring the research that has led to this publication.

Thanks are also due to Charlie Collins of DISAM, Joe Smaldone of the Department of State, Lynne Rienner and Deborah Lynes of Westview Press, and especially to those American soldiers who have taught me that modern weapons are no better than the people who fire them.

Finally, I must warn the reader that none of these aforementioned individuals or organizations is responsible for the statements, interpretations, or recommendations contained in this book. They are my own and are in no way representative of official positions or policies of the U.S. government or any of its departments or agencies.

Bruce E. Arlinghaus

1

Introduction: The Meaning of Military Development

The first duty of the sovereign, that of protecting the society from violence and invasion of other independent societies, can be performed only by means of a military force.

—Adam Smith
The Wealth of Nations, Vol. 2, p. 186

This study describes and analyzes military development—the growth and modernization of armed forces—as it is taking place in Africa. The emphasis will be on the *process* of military development, which is inevitably linked with,[1] and in many ways analogous to, the process of economic development ongoing in the region. The military situation in Africa is dynamic, a situation in which African military institutions are constantly changing in size, in scope, and in nature. As with the economic sector, the military sector's challenge to African governments is not to accelerate development but to change the nature of the process[2] such that "the first duty of the sovereign" is fulfilled without damaging the fragile economic, social, and political progress achieved since independence.

Unfortunately, not a great deal is known about the relationships between the military and other institutions in Africa. As a recent review of defense and development literature concluded, "It is remarkable how large a part of the literature on underdevelopment disregards the influence of the military sector."[3] The reasons for this lacuna are numerous, and it is not my purpose here to examine them;[4] rather this study is a first attempt at describing military influence in terms of the political and economic risks associated with military development in African nations. The concept of risks is employed because the simple measurement of costs and benefits is insufficient to explain the decisions taken by African leaders in the defense sector. It is incumbent upon them to satisfy all perceived and implied governmental functions and to balance those functions (sometimes precariously) against one another in light of resource expenditures (costs), the value of desired outcomes (benefits), and the probability that undesirable outcomes will occur (risks).

Because of the shortage of available data, previous detailed case studies, and other sources of information, calculations of costs, benefits, and risks are not analyzed here in precise terms. Rather, using fragmentary reports, statements, and the experience of economic development, an attempt has been made to outline the broad features of the process of military development, to infer its motivations, and to illustrate (in a somewhat anecdotal manner) the way in which the process so far has been manifested.

The focus is on arms transfers and the key role that they play in military development, particularly in Africa. Despite its firm understanding of what military development *ought* to be, "today's military is driven by technological inventions that have made it possible to reshape the traditional structure of the nation's armed forces."[5] Normative considerations such as national interests, strategic doctrine, and other factors to be described below become secondary as technology evolves (or in the case of Africa, is imported) and drives the processes of defense policymaking and military development.[6]

The remainder of this chapter deals with the general topic of military development: what it is and is not, and how its essentials have relevance to Africa. Chapter 2 will give a more specific background to military development in Africa. It will generally trace the process from independence to the present and emphasize the political and nonpolitical factors that have affected the direction of the process. Chapter 3 will delve into the intricacies of the arms-transfer process, give background regarding the various suppliers of arms to Africa, and sketch the roles that arms and arms suppliers play in military development.

Chapters 4, 5, and 6 are the heart of the analysis. They examine, respectively, the political economy of arms transfers, especially of those arms known as the *new conventional weapons;* the related issues of technology absorption and human resources in African militaries and societies; and the role that more appropriate military technologies could play in enhancing African military development and sovereignty. Chapter 7 summarizes the analysis and suggests its implications for U.S. security assistance policy toward Africa.

The Meaning of Military Development

Military development is an ongoing process, one that can be measured only in a relative manner. Armed forces are never totally developed or underdeveloped; instead, they are found adequate or inadequate for deterring credible threats to the security of a nation and for defending its interests when such deterrence fails.[7] Measuring adequacy is difficult since it must be determined relative to the military development of plausible threats and cannot be absolutely measured even in time of war. Given the interrelated nature of the military and society, wars may often be lost for purely political, economic, or social—rather than military—reasons.

National security is defined as "that part of government policy having as its objective the creation of national and international political conditions favorable to the protection or extension of vital national values against existing and potential adversaries."[8] In application, the concept has a narrow connotation that implies "protection of a nation's people and territories against physical assault" while also having a broader connotation of "protection, through a variety of means, of vital economic and political interests, the loss of which would threaten fundamental values and the vitality of the state."[9]

As Adam Smith's dictum quoted at the beginning of this chapter implies, national security is an *imperative* and the hallmark of the sovereign state. "The government of an independent territorial state must, by definition, have reliable instruments of coercion at its disposal to protect its people against internal and external dangers."[10] No matter how much one would like to ignore them, "our political and military traditions . . . , with the weight of almost all historical experience behind them, teach us that it is the way of the world for the earth to be divided up into independent, sovereign states, and for these states to employ war as the final arbiter for settling the disputes that arise among them."[11]

This experience has certainly not been lost on African leaders. As Leopold Senghor has said, "The need for security is a major point of national awareness in all African states."[12] "Africa shares with the United States of America, the Union of Soviet Socialist Republics and the People's Republic of China as, indeed, with the rest of the world, one common basic concern—national security,"[13] and despite the euphoria and idealism of the immediate postindependence era, realpolitik and older notions of statecraft have taken root in Africa.[14]

But at the same time as "intervention by one African state's army in another's problems made its appearance in the late 1970s and has since increased,"[15] "every corner of Africa faces conflicts that, if not eliminated or at least dampened, represent permanent drains of funds otherwise available for development."[16] These conditions confront African leaders with a dilemma, elucidated in several forums by Robert S. McNamara, former U.S. secretary of defense and former president of the World Bank: "In a modernizing society security means development. Security is not military hardware, though it may include it; security is not military force, though it may involve it; security is not traditional military activity, though it may encompass it. Security is development, and without development there can be no security."[17] This linkage between military and economic development should be recognized and accepted as such, because "most nonwestern leaders do not distinguish between development and security issues. They see expenditures on armaments and expenditures for economic development not as mutually exclusive alternatives, but as mutually complementary necessities."[18]

Although there is some controversy as to whether economic development actually promotes political stability,[19] there is no denying that the security issues confronting developing, and especially African, nations are fundamentally different from those faced by developed countries. Although the defense-versus-development dilemma can be interpreted as representing the narrow and broad meanings of national security, African states—as new nations—are concerned with establishing national capacities taken for granted by the developed world. These capacities include:

- Managing domestic processes of economic development and national integration
- Resisting outside penetration
- Dominating regional competitors
- Deterring outside states from rendering aid to those competitors
- Achieving autarky in critical weapons systems, or being able to bargain successfully for them during crises
- Developing a national awareness of, and desire to increase, the relative strength and influence of the state[20]

In Africa, these goals are also identified with governmental, as well as national, survival[21] and are articulated with a distinctively African twist. For example, Nigeria's national security goals include:

- Defense of sovereignty, independence, and territorial integrity
- Creation of the economic and political conditions in Africa and throughout the world necessary to foster national self-reliance and rapid economic development
- Promotion of equality and self-reliance in Africa and the rest of the developing world
- Promotion of social justice and human dignity everywhere, especially for black people
- Commitment to the United Nations, world peace, international security, nonalignment, and the fight against racism in South Africa[22]

The military plays four vital roles in the pursuit of national security in developing countries. First, it is a mark of national sovereignty. Second, it is charged with external security, protecting the nation from outside threats to its territory and interests. Third, it maintains internal security, in lieu of or in conjunction with existing police forces. Finally, it engages in "nation-building" or civic-action activities that either enhance its relations with society or at best keep it busy during peacetime.[23] As an institution, the military is linked to the broader society and the national security policy process through the formulation of defense policy and specific defense planning to carry it out.[24] Defense planning includes five steps.[25]

Specifying Purposes. This step should begin the process. It includes definitions of national values and interests, together with a specification of those that are vital, important, or secondary. The setting of priorities is critical, because it permits planners to calculate costs, benefits, and risks in an informed manner.

Appraising Opposition. Which adversaries have the means and motivation to place defined national interests in jeopardy? What are the bases for threats—are they realistic or imaginary, are they potential or actual? Just as interests should be given priorities, threats also should be arrayed in a hierarchy.

Formulating Strategy. This step, together with the next, is principally a military function and forms the core of the process of military development. This is where military professionalism, expertise, and experience are needed to insure that adequate, appropriate means are acquired or developed to protect national security.

Allocating Resources. Military development is not an unconstrained process. It is limited by available resources and the necessary balance between military and other needs. It is at this point that the greatest political and economic risks are taken—forced upon decisionmakers by circumstances beyond their immediate control.

Reconciling Ends with Means. At this point, military development feeds back into the national security process. Issues of trade-offs between defense and development, militarism, nepotism, bureaucratic infighting, and so on become prominent. To be too parsimonious in defense is to lose the nation (or power); to be too generous is to retard development and thus jeopardize stability and long-term national interests.

These considerations will be implicit in much of the description and analysis of the political economy of arms transfers, whereas discussions of technology transfer and absorption will deal with factors of infrastructure and human resources. Military development can thus be examined at three levels:

Strategic level: the armed forces of a nation secure the objectives of national policy by applying force or the threat of force

Operational level: available military resources are applied to attain specific goals or counter specific threats

Tactical level: specific techniques are used by small units or individuals to carry out the directives generated at high levels[26]

At the operational and tactical levels, military development has four essential parts: force structure, modernization, sustainability, and readiness. *Force structure* includes the size, organization, and composition of the armed forces. *Modernization* includes military technology in its broadest sense—both equipment and knowledge—and drives the development process at these levels. *Sustainability* refers to the capacity of the organization and culture to absorb, operate, maintain, and support equipment and personnel. *Readiness* is a measure of the ability of the force to carry out its assigned missions, both in deterrence and defense.[27]

Taken together, these factors—as they are manifested in human resources (technical skills, leadership, morale, unit cohesion), logistics (supply and maintenance), mobility (rapid movement of troops and equipment, projection of power outside national boundaries), firepower (quantity and quality of arms), manpower (number of personnel under arms, level of organization), and command and control (communications facilities and administrative expertise)—all add up to military capability or the product of military development.[28] Again, these are dynamic and relative variables, constantly changing the relative balance of military power in a region.

The evidence indicates that military development is occurring in Africa;[29] at issue is whether military capability has improved, relative to the threats and needs of African states. As will be described below, the demand for arms is primarily politically driven,[30] but there is little that supplier nations can do directly to control or change the nature of military development in Africa.[31] These trends begin ultimately with the national security perceptions of African leaders, made operational through the defense planning process. The outcome, although military in form, more often than not is a reflection of economic and political concerns.

Myths and Risks of Military Development

Although to students of defense planning military development would intuitively appear to be a part of the overall process of national development, it is frequently one of the most misunderstood phenomena associated with the nation-state. Because military institutions and the military profession are so highly specialized and to a degree divorced from the society of which they are a part, the casual observer and the political analyst alike often fail to understand their nature and the activity that takes place within them.

In this section, five of the most common myths associated with military development are examined. The term *myth* is used because they are attempts by analysts to explain how a state of events has occurred—in fact rationalizing them—without reference to a firm empirical base. In addition to factual shortcomings, these explanations are mythical because for the analyst they have become reality. In the absence of data, the proponents of these myths have substituted what is at best intuition, at worst ideology. As a result, much of true analytical and descriptive value has been lost in the polemics associated with the politics of social science. As one analyst has put it, "Research on the issue of security and development has been grounded in the ideological assumptions of the authors."[32]

The five myths of military development are:

- That the military are political modernizers
- That the military are nation builders
- That militarism is rampant
- That disarmament will lead to development
- That new conventional weapons will revolutionize military development

The first two myths, which emphasize the positive aspects of military development, are most commonly espoused by those who would seek to look on the brighter side of the authoritarian regimes so common in the Third World. The second set of myths is the opposite of those preceding and sees only evil inherent in the process of military development. The fifth myth is espoused by those at both ends of the political spectrum, who see new conventional weapons as a panacea that will insure both political stability and economic development in the Third World.

Each myth possesses an element of truth, which, unfortunately, is often lost in the debate that surrounds it and its opposite. In addition, each myth lends itself to the simplistic interpretation of highly complex political, military, and economic issues. In this sense, the myths of military development are often counterproductive, distorting issues and disguising more critical facts that pertain to the security and welfare of developing nations.

It would be preferable to deal with the underlying facts in terms of the risks they pose for developing countries that are trying to cope with the problems of political modernization, nation building, militarism, and economic development in concrete, rather than abstract and ideological, terms. The leaders of the developing nations are faced with a real dilemma of trying to solve all of these problems while at the same time providing for the security of their citizens and their common interests. This is no easy task, given the conflicting and competing demands for their attention and scarce resources. It is in this context that the last myth is so critical—precisely because it seems to offer an apparently easy solution to the problems of military development, regardless of the ideological orientation of the regime involved.

The Military as Political Modernizers

The perception of the military as the modernizing force in the developing world—and in Africa in particular—enjoyed great popularity in scholarly circles in the late 1950s and early 1960s.[33] Most analysts focused on the "role" of the military in development, especially its participation in political modernization and nation building. The latter will be discussed in more detail below, in terms of the particular myth associated with it; the supposed ability and potential of the military to perform as political modernizers will be analyzed here.

In the newly independent, multiethnic states of the developing world, soldiers rapidly became embroiled in domestic politics, unlike their counterparts in the developed world. The United States and other Western nations thus have been confronted with the difficult situation of dealing with soldiers as heads of state or with military regimes that had come to power through coups d'etat, something that violates Western norms of civil-military relations. These rulers and regimes were perceived, at best, as undemocratic (if not authoritarian), and some justification was necessary for continued relations with and recognition of them. That justification emerged as the myth of the military as political modernizers— the most acceptable rationale for dealing with soldiers as rulers. Given the unstable and often chaotic nature of politics and political change in the developing world, military leaders were often seen as godsends— each one viewed as a potential Cincinnatus or Ataturk who would establish order in the new states, then retire to his barracks and to the established and accepted role of the military as protector of the nation from *external* threats. It was precisely because they were soldiers that the leaders were best qualified for this role. The military establishment as an institution—not its members—was perceived as the only source of talent for national leadership. For example, "African armies tend to be the most detribalized, Westernized, modernized, integrated, and cohesive institutions in their respective states. The army is usually the most disciplined agency in the state. It often enjoys a greater sense of national identity than other institutions. In other skills, including the capacity to coerce and to communicate, the army is the most modernized agency in the country."[34]

As these modernized agencies, therefore, the armies of Africa and elsewhere found themselves rapidly drawn into a political vacuum created by the failure of civilian rule to maintain order and to accomplish the goals of national development.[35] As Claude Welch has indicated, "Few political parties in Africa, for example, can match the centralization, discipline, hierarchy, esprit de corps, and speed of communications manifested by even the smallest professional armies on the continent. Qualitatively, the organizational strength of the military sets it apart from other groups."[36]

But there is little empirical evidence to support the contention that such qualities necessarily qualify military leaders for national office. As Eric Nordlinger has said, the modernizers "have presented remarkably little evidence for their arguments, while failing to analyze—as opposed to simply stating—the supposed connection between the officers' technical orientations and social backgrounds and their hypothesized modernizing activities and motivations."[37]

Other analysts of military regimes, including Claude Welch and Morris Janowitz, question the relevance of military skills for political leadership. Although they do not deny that some skills are readily transferable to the civilian sector, they doubt the sufficiency of such skills for doing a better job than civilian counterparts.[38] In fact, recent research indicates that the African military is not apolitical, that distinctions of civilian regime versus military regime are useless, that military professionalism is dubious at best, and that each nation has developed its own style of military behavior.[39]

The Military as Nation Builders

This myth is composed of two parts, both pertaining to the alleged contribution of the military to economic development. The first part deals with the impact of military spending on economic growth; the second imputes contributions to human resources and infrastructure through technical training and civic-action projects.

Perhaps the best-known and most-discussed study of the economic effects of military spending is the one done in the early 1970s by Emile Benoit for the U.S. Arms Control and Disarmament Agency. His findings are summarized as follows:

> There were indications of some favorable growth effects of defense expenditures, on a gross basis. Defense manpower training created strengthened attitudes and skills useful in civilian occupations, and the defense

programs provided dual-use infrastructure and other goods and services similar to those provided by the civilian economy. An observed association between high defense burdens, high rates of price increase, and high growth rates . . . also suggested the likelihood that in some countries defense expenditures may have had a "Keynesian" type of effect in stimulating the use of unemployed or underemployed resources by raising aggregate demand, where anti-inflation policies would otherwise have kept it below the level conducive to maximum real growth. Up to a certain level, defense programs also contributed to the essential security required for economic progress, and under conditions of national danger may even have had energizing and motivational benefits.

Devoting resources to high grade civilian investment projects rather than to defense might, of course, have produced even more growth. However, even here the practically relevant consideration is not the *optimum* alternative use of the resources, but the probable *actual* alternative use. The probable actual alternative use of the resources absorbed by defense programs is a mix of civilian consumption with slight growth effects, civilian investment projects with widely varying growth effects, and no use at all—that is, a higher rate of unemployment of resources. (emphasis in original)[40]

Much of the criticism of Benoit is ideological in content (and is summarized below as the myth of disarmament and development). But some valid criticisms of his assumptions, data, and methodology can be, and have been, made.[41] However, several recent restudies, using more extensive, disaggregated data and more sophisticated techniques, have essentially validated his findings.[42] What these studies have revealed is what Benoit reiterated in a later response to his critics, that "the main determinant of the size of the defense burden was the expectation of political and military leaders of the need for forces to deter, to threaten or to engage in combat" and that "money is not spent on defense just because it happens to be available: there are always competing needs, and the military, like other claimants, must justify its claims."[43]

A recent study by two analysts at the U.S. Naval Postgraduate School, using a sample of ninety countries for 1970–1978 revealed that by disaggregating the sample into resource-rich and -poor developing countries, it was possible to explain a number of significant trends in defense expenditures. The resource-rich countries essentially have sufficient resources to pay for both defense and development—and do so. The poorer nations tend to have much lower expenditures relative to gross domestic product (GDP) because they are resource constrained and face government budget cuts. Although income shifts, waste, and opportunity costs might indicate that defense cuts would be appropriate, usually it is development projects that are reduced. The reasons are very simple:

Military expenditures are current outlays (not including arms bought on credit), whereas development projects are future growth, and there is a natural tendency to try to maintain the status quo. As a result, military budgets in poor countries are not reduced, but are frozen and will be expanded as the economy strengthens. The beneficial side effects of military expenditures usually are realized only by those nations whose militaries are sufficiently developed to make such contributions to nation building.[44]

Thus the criticisms of military spending as a growth inhibitor are not empirically justified. But is the reverse necessarily true, as claimed by the supporters of nation building? There is evidence that such infrastructural and skill spillovers as do occur are incidental,[45] especially in Africa. Military civic-action projects are usually undertaken to keep the military busy or out of the way, as an adjunct to military operations, or worse, instead of training.[46]

Although in an ideal sense "the acculturative process in the army tends to be focused on acquiring technical skills that are of particular value for economic development,"[47] that soldiers

> can transfer their technical-managerial skills from the military to the economic sphere is an open question at best, especially since these usually derive from the handling of military organization, logistics and equipment of World War II vintage. They may very well be able to do so with regard to routine administrative matters, but it is doubtful that transferability occurs with regard to the far more complex, specialized and demanding sphere of economic and financial decision making.[48]

In fact, as will be discussed below, as the weapons imported into Africa become more sophisticated, the military becomes a consumer of increasingly scarce educated and skilled labor. Another consideration is cost. Many African states developed national youth service organizations with Israeli and other assistance. Most were failures, both as military and as educational projects, because they were unable to do either very well. The defense or paramilitary training that members received was minimal, and the skills training they received cost three times as much as comparable training in schools.[49]

The problem with the myth of nation building is that it ignores the primary function of the military—national defense—and attempts to justify military expenditures or assistance as "very important nation-building efforts."[50] Even though the military can make contributions to development on an exceptional basis, as when Zimbabwean army trucks recently were used to help move a bumper crop of maize to market,[51] such activities are secondary missions.

Those nations, such as Tanzania, that have emphasized the development role over the defense role have had rude awakenings when engaged in conflicts[52] and have had to reassess their defense programs.[53] Military resources should be devoted to training in military skills—and the military should not be used as a substitute for sound government and private-sector educational and development programs. Just as a construction company is not a military organization, a military unit is not a construction enterprise. Each one has its own functions and capabilities, not to be confused with the other.

Militarism Rampant

This myth is perhaps the most politically loaded of all. It focuses on the performance of military regimes and the growth of arms transfers and military expenditures that they allegedly produce. Inevitably, links to external suppliers (usually in the West) are cited as evidence of some sort of international conspiracy to promote dependency, repression, and support of reactionary regimes.[54]

The literature of militarism is quite extensive.[55] It can be summarized here by indicating that its proponents almost inevitably dismiss the merits of modernizing proposals[56] and instead offer an argument that there exists a coordinated imperialist strategy to keep military control of African regimes.[57] Allegedly the principal means of accomplishing this is the Military Assistance Program (of the most commonly cited culprit—the United States).[58] This argument may be faulted on several counts,[59] not the least of which is its inherent bias against the West and in favor of the the Soviet bloc.

The second issue is one of definition. Most of the antimilitarist group fail to discriminate between true military regimes, rulers who have emerged through military coups, and mixed regimes. An excellent example of this is labeling Mobutu in Zaire as a military ruler.[60] True, he came to power while a soldier and may be considered to be an authoritarian. But he is no more supported or protected by the military than by any other major class or institution in the country. In fact, evidence indicates that he purposely keeps the army weak, fragmented, and dispersed over the countryside because it represents the greatest *threat* to his regime![61] The evidence is quite strong that African military leaders are no more or less ideologically committed to the West or East than are civilians[62] and that the dominant trend is for postcoup regimes to be mixed civilian and military groups,[63] more concerned with solving common economic problems[64] than with repressing their populations or making war.[65]

The measure of militarism rampant must be taken in two ways. First, is the frequency of coups increasing? And, second, what do soldiers do once they seize power? Except for the "revolutionary" coups that occur repeatedly in several countries such as Ghana, it appears that the frequency of coups is abating in the region.[66] But more important than the apparent military reluctance to engage in political action is the willingness to turn over power to civilian rule.[67] Their economic performance has been as good, or as bad, as that of their civilian counterparts,[68] and they have been as politically fragmented, reflecting the same cleavages as their societies.[69] But what is more important, they have *not* increased military expenditures significantly.[70]

Rather than *militarism* becoming rampant, *militarization* of interstate relations in Africa has increased.[71] This is reflected in the increase in conflict and consequent demand for military development in the region. And as the studies cited above regarding military expenditures indicate, when nations feel threatened by their neighbors, they often forget budgetary concerns. Whether this phenomenon constitutes an "African arms race"[72] is problematic, but it surely will mean an increase in African military development.

Development Through Disarmament

It seems fundamentally wrong for developing nations to spend money on arms while so many basic human needs go unmet in their countries. Equally, it seems misguided for developed countries to sell arms to developing nations (or provide them with arms) instead of spending additional monies for development assistance. But while one can sympathize with such a position, it is extremely difficult to put into operation any plan that might effectively change the way nations—both those supplying and those receiving arms—behave.

Such international bodies as the Brandt Commission[73] and the United Nations (UN)[74] have conducted extended studies regarding the relationship between disarmament and development and have reached essentially the same conclusion: A new international economic order can only be paid for with monies freed through world disarmament. Despite its apparent merits, this argument is essentially flawed because it presumes a zero-sum world, in which every defense expenditure automatically incurs opportunity costs in development, it assumes that sovereign nations would be willing to forgo military force as a means of resolving disputes, and it confuses defense and disarmament.

The issue of opportunity costs, discussed above in reference to nation building, deserves restatement: Even assuming a willingness on the part of African nations to demand only development assistance, there is no guarantee that those monies would be efficiently spent. Funds could just as easily be siphoned off from development projects as from defense endeavors. To make opportunity costs realizable, one must have perfect environmental conditions, including human behavior. Equally idealistic is the notion that nations would subordinate sovereignty to a world government, which through its deliberations would settle all disputes fairly and amicably. Even those nations most likely to benefit from a new international economic order jealously guard their newly won sovereignty and would view such a scheme as a conspiracy by the superpowers to dominate them.

This points up the disarmament/defense distinction. While many nonaligned and developing countries want *nuclear* disarmament, they also "emphasize the incontestability of the right of States to legitimate defense and national security as well as the right of colonial peoples to use the means available to them, including arms, to achieve and secure their freedom and independence."[75]

This contradiction is further compounded by the intensity of belief in the myth of development through disarmament. So many development schemes have failed, it seems that the only solution is more and more money, available only through disarmament of the superpowers. But as one analyst has pointed out, this hope is unfounded: "A conventional illusion among most developing countries is the hope that if by some miracle general and complete disarmament should come about, vast resources would be released for aiding world development. . . . There are no firm indications that the release of such resources would ever lead to the diversion of these resources toward socially-oriented development in some of the disarming countries."[76]

New Conventional Weapons

This final myth is espoused by both left and right and is perhaps the most pervasive and insidious, since it offers a simplistic panacea for complex defense problems in both developed and developing countries. It will be discussed in detail in each of the subsequent chapters, as the focus of the risks of arms transfers, and so will only be generally discussed here.

New conventional weapons (NCW) are purported to "revolutionize warfare" and are offered as examples of how "technology will save us,"[77] both in Europe and in the Third World. They are heralded as being cost-effective, allowing individual soldiers to destroy million-dollar tanks and single missiles to down multi-million-dollar aircraft or sink billion-dollar ships.[78] In addition, these weapons systems are claimed to be easy to operate and to maintain, allowing armies to substitute technology for manpower.[79] Even the left has espoused them:

> PGMs [precision-guided munitions] could be cheaply mass-produced in great quantities and operated by relatively unskilled soldiers. Manned

vehicles, used for launching PGMs and transporting soldiers, could be small, agile, and easy to conceal. Instead of the cumbersome, weapons system based organisation, with its complex and vulnerable support systems and its oversophisticated and vulnerable centralized command system, armed forces could be organised in small dispersed mobile units, on the basis of decentralized authority.[80]

These systems are so appealing because they appear to be cheap, they do not require a militaristic, professional army, and they lend themselves readily to territorial defense schemes,[81] with part-time, people's armies. But the mythical images of "dumb soldiers operating smart bombs" or the humble freedom fighter shooting down a jet with his SAM-7 are illusory, for a number of reasons.[82]

New Conventional Weapons Are Not Cheap. They usually are very expensive, high-technology systems that require elaborate support facilities, highly skilled maintenance personnel, and delivery means far more complex than a simple truck.[83]

They Are Really Not That Simple. Both research and experience indicate that while the concept of operation for these systems is simple, the psychomotor skills needed to operate them and the resources needed to develop and maintain those skills are significantly more than the myth suggests.[84]

The Economic Distortions of Financial and Human Resources Caused by NCW Are Much Larger than Imagined. Because NCW are deceptively expensive, require skilled human resources, and are just not that dependable,[85] even the United States is experiencing difficulties paying for and absorbing them. If the richest nation in the world, with virtually 100 percent literacy, cannot do so, how can a poor nation with low literacy rates be expected to?

Conclusions

These myths, taken together, form the basis for misunderstandings of the process of military development. The following analysis does not debate the normative appropriateness of military forces in Africa; it takes them and their development as a given. It does not argue that military expenditures are intrinsically good; rather it recognizes that African nations will spend money on defense. What this analysis does attempt is an examination of the process of military development as it has occurred so far in Africa and an evaluation of its appropriateness, its motivations, its successes and failures. In short, it attempts to determine if the money being spent on defense is being spent well, and whether in so doing African armed forces are capable of accomplishing their first responsibility, preservation of their national security.

2
Military Development
in an African Context

In ancient times the opulent and civilized found it difficult to defend themselves against the poor and barbarous nations. In modern times the poor and barbarous find it difficult to defend themselves against the opulent and civilized.

—Adam Smith
The Wealth of Nations, Vol. 2, p. 202

As the first twenty-five years of African independence draw to a close, the results of the process of military development are seen to be significant changes in the nature and form of African armed forces. What were little more than constabulary forces twenty-five years ago have become in some cases emerging regional military powers, responding not only to internal security needs but also to increasing external threats.

African militaries have evolved from lightly armed infantry units into mechanized forces and emerging air and sea forces. Through the acquisition of sophisticated conventional weapons, some of these forces are developing potential combat capabilities that compare favorably with those of the industrialized nations supplying the weapons.[1] These arms transfers, together with the doubling of African military expenditures every five years[2] and the presence of foreign troops in increasing numbers,[3] will determine the course of African military development over the next quarter century.

The growth and modernization of African military forces may be attributed directly to several political developments in the region and the conflicts they have engendered. These include the continued challenge of South Africa, the leading military force in the region; the failure of the Organization of African Unity (OAU) to effect cooperation and defuse conflict and competition among its member states; and the failure of African states to peacefully manage political and economic affairs within their own boundaries.[4]

This dynamic, more threatening environment confronts the African military forces with a series of challenges that go beyond their traditional responsibility for national defense. They must deal with the expansion and development of their own institutions. They must resolve internal cleavages that mirror those of their societies, but threaten their integration and effectiveness as armed forces. They must deal with the aftermath of conflicts—absorbing surrendered enemy troops from civil wars and demobilizing unneeded troops in the wake of victory or defeat. They must continue to define their proper role in the economic-development and political-modernization processes, finding ways to contribute to them yet remove themselves from direct interference or participation. Finally, they must, by their professionalism and capability, deter or defuse potential conflicts, whether internal or external in origin.[5]

These are not easy tasks, considering the constrained economic base from which these militaries must operate and the fragile political environments in which they must survive. Yet perform them they must, in order to function as military institutions and to effectively direct the course of military development in their societies. Although arms transfers will play a critical role in this process of development, ultimately it is political and economic forces that shape weapons acquisition decisions, in terms not only of what arms will be procured but also of how their costs will be paid.

The remainder of this chapter describes the context from which African armed forces have emerged, analyzes the sources of conflict in the region, and suggests the forms that the challenges described above may take.

The Colonial Legacy

The characteristics of the past quarter century of African military development have been determined largely by the immediately preceding colonial era.[6] Of certain significance were the effects of the initial colonial conquest and subjugation, which led directly to what Mazrui has termed the "decline of the warrior tradition."[7] By this he refers to the fact that in traditional African societies, all men were warriors and military virtues were extolled. With the colonial period, traditional Africa was demilitarized, and Western military traditions were substituted both within ranks and in the larger society. As a result, many educated Africans disdain military service and seek to subordinate a military that may in fact be technically superior. This has created a tension in civil-military relations, leading to the military's often becoming a competing political elite in African societies.[8]

The second major effect was the use of selective recruiting of "martial races" for the armed forces, so that loyalty could be assured by exploiting tribal and ethnic rivalries.[9] As the colonial armies were most often used to subjugate their own peoples, this development had the effect of alienating the colonial military from the general population. With independence, many armed forces lacked well-defined roles in the new states, were identified with the former colonial powers, and thus seemed largely irrelevant in the new regimes.

Third, each colonial power had its own military traditions and practices, many of which were handed on to and retained by African armed forces. For instance, the British recruited volunteers to serve locally and maintain internal order, with African troops serving overseas only during World War II. The French, on the other hand, recruited volunteers for their overseas army, with African troops serving in both world wars. Over 181,000 saw service on the Western Front in 1914–1918. The Belgians created the Force Publique in the 1930s, providing a pool of mechanics, technicians, and craftsmen. The Portuguese used white troops until after World War I, then recruited significant numbers of blacks, only to shift back to whites again during the insurgencies of the 1960s and 1970s.

These actions have had an important role in establishing the public image and traditions of the military. Even more important was the tendency for colonial powers to clone African forces in their own likenesses and to inculcate attitudes and standards of professionalism, such as the British belief in an apolitical army, regardless of their appropriateness to an African setting.[10]

In addition, there was a tendency to create additional paramilitary and sizable police forces to supplement the military in its defense role. The military, in turn, would support these units in their maintenance of internal security. Very often these militias, general service units, and police forces are organized and equipped in much the same manner as the military, which subsequently leads to confusion over responsibility and control for performing missions of internal security, external defense, and peacekeeping. Such confusion escalates during extraordinary situations such as mutiny, coup, or insurgency,[11] especially since many of these supplementary forces are larger than the military and equally well armed.[12]

Finally, because of these strong traditions and a series of military agreements concluded prior to independence, the influence of the former colonial powers tended to persist among African militaries.[13] Subsequent events, however, have introduced alternative models for African military development (most notably those of the United States and the Soviet Union and its allies) in the form of military assistance agreements.[14] These linkages provide African nations with arms and training of foreign origin with which to modernize their forces and deal with postindependence conflicts. But the agreements also have introduced into the region significant numbers of military and technical advisors, and in some instances (the French and Cubans) foreign troops have been stationed on African soil.

Because of the highly political and strategic nature of these agreements, many African nations find themselves diversifying their sources of military development aid in much the same way that they are, in the name of nonalignment, accepting economic assistance from all who offer it. While this may be politically shrewd, as will be discussed in subsequent chapters, it can have a devastating effect on the process of military development. It often causes larger and more modern forces to be less capable than those preceding them.

The military itself remains somewhat ambiguous about its proper role in a developing economy. Many critics (and soldiers) appear to feel that in the absence of conflict, civic action is better than no action.[15] But since many African armies are poorly trained and disciplined to begin with,[16] the costs of such activities to military development should be weighed to determine whether or not they are appropriate.

Increasing Conflict

Clearly the threats confronting African nations have changed, as manifested in the increase of conflict since the immediate postindependence era.[17] These threats have taken the form of civil wars, expansionist nationalism and irredentism, foreign intervention, and transborder military intervention.[18]

Foremost among the causes of African interstate conflicts are boundaries—the legacy of the colonial era, made without reference to natural or cultural considerations.[19] Although some of these disputes appear to be amenable to negotiation,[20] nevertheless, as Samora Machel has said, "There are two things you cannot choose—brothers and neighbors. We can't move our country."[21] Since many of these boundaries cut across natural resources and access routes, the possibility of an "African resource war" between African states is much more likely than is direct superpower intervention in the region.[22]

Internal threats originate from four sources: (1) continuing economic failure in the face of a burgeoning population (as one African official has stated, "I don't know of anything that brings down a government faster than hungry people"[23]); (2) problems of political succession, from charismatic leaders as well as from military regimes;[24] (3) a growing unconventional warfare threat, with insurgents operating from cross-border sanctuaries, and—perhaps more important—the threat posed by national liberation movements using another state as a base (the "Laos-Lebanon" syndrome);[25] and (4) the military itself, especially in the lower ranks as some soldiers are forcibly demobilized and those remaining in service perceive that they are not receiving adequate pay, housing, and so on.[26]

The final source of African conflict has been the failure of the OAU to mediate ongoing disputes between African states,[27] to effect a satisfactory degree of regional defense cooperation,[28] and to mount an effective African peacekeeping force,[29] which would provide the means for enforcing its mediating efforts and form the operational basis for an African defense force.[30]

Conclusions

Nowhere is the need for cooperation greater than in what Cynthia Enloe has called the "super-ethnic" armed forces,[31] African navies and air forces. Because of the recent Law of the Sea decisions regarding territorial waters, and the extensive coastlines and rivers of the region, African nations have an even greater incentive to develop their sea forces and to find means of naval cooperation. Since many of the border conflicts mentioned above have taken place on the water, and much of Africa's oil and other mineral wealth lies offshore, the requirements for maritime surveillance and patrol have increased dramatically.[32]

Even though many of these missions could also be performed by aircraft, the astronomical costs of both ships and planes are such that no single country, except perhaps Nigeria and South Africa, can realistically expect to do so alone. This would be an excellent area of military cooperation, but it is encumbered by the simple fact that those nations most likely to benefit from such arrangements are those currently in conflict with each other—neighbors.

Other opportunities for cooperation exist in joint aircraft procurement and the establishment of regional training facilities.[33] Yet again, because of the inability and unwillingness of African states to agree on common aircraft types and because potential enemies may find themselves mutually dependent for training and logistical support, such efforts have failed.

This failure of interstate cooperation is not surprising, since it is a rare event when services *within* an African nation's armed forces cooperate with one another.[34] Thus, the path of African military development is likely to be more competitive than cooperative. Decreasing rationality and efficiency can be expected at two levels: within the region and within individual states as they seek varied alternative sources of military technology and development.

3
Sources and Scope
of African Arms Transfers

The great change introduced into the art of war by the invention of fire-arms, has enhanced still further both the expence of exercising and disciplining any particular number of soldiers in time of peace, and that of employing them in time of war. Both their arms and their ammunition are become more expensive.

—Adam Smith
The Wealth of Nations, Vol. 2, p. 201

Virtually all African nations (South Africa is the most notable exception) are totally dependent upon the industrialized nations for arms and other forms of military technology.[1] This situation dates from precolonial times, when firearms were imported across the Sahara and along the coast, and persists to this day. Africa has never developed a significant indigenous arms production capacity.

Even traditional weapons manufactured by African iron makers and artisans were quickly displaced (from the late precolonial period into colonial times) by trade goods of European or Asian manufacture, which were mass-produced at lower cost and flooded the local market.[2] Although some items were of superior quality—such as those made of steel, rather than iron—European weapons were not especially good. This was particularly true of firearms. The patterns of the trade in nineteenth-century arms and armaments established a situation that persists to this day, including unfavorable conditions of trade, inferior quality of imported guns, a diversity of weapons with an attendant difficulty in obtaining compatible ammunition and replacement parts, a shortage of skilled local repairmen and facilities, and a lack of regular training in gun handling, marksmanship, and tactics.[3]

With the advent of the colonial era, of course, the trade in arms was closely controlled and monitored, insuring the colonial powers a monopoly of military force. Institution of a Pax Colonia reduced demand for arms in local conflicts, and African military forces were created only in the service of the colonial power to maintain order, quell uprisings, and collect taxes. In particular, Africans were not permitted access to knowledge of more sophisticated weapons, especially those that allowed a minute white population to control and exploit masses of blacks:

> As was common at this time [the late nineteenth century], almost all the troops used in this campaign were Africans, only the officers being British. One of the most important duties of these officers was to operate the Maxim guns. It would clearly be too dangerous to teach natives, even though they might be wearing a British uniform, the secrets of the white man's ultimate weapon. . . . Once again one sees the central place of the machine gun in the Africans' analysis of the reasons for their conquest and subjugation. . . . The Europeans jealously guarded both the machine guns themselves and the secrets of their operation.[4]

This secretiveness on the part of Europeans is a large part of the legacy of colonial times to the contemporary armies of Africa, but it only partially explains the growing demand for arms in the region. It is important to note that although the arms trade in precolonial and colonial times may be interpreted as just another facet of European exploitation of Africa, that is not the case today. Despite the thinking of many *dependencia* theorists and those who adhere to the myth of militarism rampant (discussed in Chapter 1), the "pull factors," or reasons for which African nations demand arms, are clearly stronger than the "push," or supply, factors on the part of the industrialized, arms-producing nations.[5]

Arms Transfers and Foreign Policy

The primary motivation of the arms suppliers is the desire to achieve political influence in the increasingly important, yet fragmented regions of the developing world. Recognizing the demand for arms as an opportunity to achieve this goal, the industrialized nations often compete without regard to long-term consequences. In fact, arms transfers have become, in many ways, the principal instrument of foreign policy in the Third World.

A senior White House official was quoted in a recent *Time* magazine article on U.S. foreign policy as having said, "Our foreign policy is in large part arms sales; that's true. Every other week we are selling something to someone."[6] Despite recognition that world military expenditures far exceed those for foreign economic aid,[7] the leaders of the industrialized nations feel compelled to use whatever means are available to implement their foreign-policy goals, including arms transfers. This "waging politics with arms sales"[8] has created a situation in which international relations may very well be considered isomorphic with arms transfers. As Andrew J. Pierre has recently written, "Arms sales have become, more now than ever before, a crucial dimension of world politics. They are now major strands in the warp and woof of international affairs. Arms sales are far more than an economic occurrence, a military relationship or an arms control challenge—*arms sales are foreign policy writ large*" (emphasis in original).[9]

Arms transfers are generally considered as part of the broad category of military aid and assistance, which includes equipment, training, spares, and ammunition[10] and

> embraces such activities as the provision of advice, deployment of training cadres, creation of schools and individual instruction, the latter both abroad and in the home training establishments of the provider. It is in increasing demand as emerging countries acquire sophisticated weapons, and ranges from the provision of one or two junior officers and a few instructional courses to the involvement of senior officers and consultancy teams in advising on the reorganization and re-equipment of complete armed forces.
>
> It is, in short, an attempt to make up for a lack of indigenous experience. Assistance shades into military support when the recipient is unable to manage the business in hand and significant numbers of military personnel on loan assume executive positions, but the distinction is sometimes no more than academic. Military support may involve the deployment of units such as engineers and supporting technical services, pending the establishment of indigenous facilities in fields where education and training are at a premium, but it should not be confused with military intervention, involving provision of combatant troops on a significant scale. Military assistance and support are inevitably associated with defence sales, the military tending to shop where they are trained and vice versa. Assistance often includes subsidised sales or gifts of equipment, but the apparent generosity of the donor seldom extends to free after-sales service and cut-price or free equipment, possibly obsolescent in the first place, sometimes become more of a hindrance than a help.[11]

Experience has shown, however, that arms transfers form the most significant portion of military assistance in terms of both financial expenditure and political influence. Increasingly these transfers have come to shape all other aspects of military aid and assistance, since the acquisition of weapons systems determines the form and scope of military growth and modernization in recipient countries.[12]

Military development in Africa, compared to that of other regions in the developing world such as the Middle East, may appear to be somewhat retarded, but it has in fact been accelerating since independence. African military expenditures and arms acquisitions have been doubling roughly every five years since 1960, and the arms trade with Africa has continued to increase steadily throughout the past decade. Although arms purchases peaked in 1978 and appear to have declined somewhat,[13] the overall trend both in purchases and deliveries has been to increase dramatically the amount of military equipment supplied to African nations. (See Table 3 in the Statistical Appendix.)

In addition to the strong demand factors existing in the African political environment, significant changes in the perceptions of supplier nations affect their perspectives on Africa as a potential market for arms. Although Africa has often occupied a secondary position in global politics, in particular with regard to the superpowers, the strategic importance of Africa as a supplier of critical resources and its location astride sea and air lines of communication have changed this role dramatically.[14] There is growing recognition that, as Lenin has said, "whoever holds Africa holds Europe" and America as well,[15] and this has only served to accelerate supplier responses to African demands for arms.

In addition to the growing frequency and ferocity of conflict in the region, there is a growing demand for military development in Africa as part of the overall process of growth and modernization. As pointed out in the preceding chapter, African military institutions at independence were little more than constabulary forces. In the face of growing internal and external threats, they have been found wanting both in capability and deterrent value. Although domestic defense expenditures in Africa represent only a minute fraction of the world total, the trend toward military development has caused the region to become a major importer of arms and military technology.[16]

The extreme economic problems of the region not only make for increased conflict and instability (thus stimulating the demand for arms) but also make the political influence that supplier nations hope to gain just that much more available. Most African nations cannot afford to purchase arms on anything less than the most concessionary credit or grant-aid terms. These concessions or gifts have political costs, making military aid and assistance even more potent instruments of political influence. Unlike the Middle East, where the buyers of weapons control the market through high demand and excess petrodollars, African nations must seek the best weapons at the lowest financial cost. The difference between dollars and defense is often made up by concessions of political influence to suppliers.

But there are potential costs and benefits for both recipients and suppliers of arms. They may be summarized as follows:[17] First, arms provided to allies may enhance their internal security and external defense, but they may also exacerbate regional tensions and lead to conflict and internal discord. Second, arms transfers to one side of a regional conflict may restore a local balance of power and thus deter external aggression. They may also, however, lead to local arms races that could lead to war as neighboring nations feel threatened or feel the need for preemptive military action to retain or restore regional dominance. Third, although arms transfers may provide suppliers with a means of political influence with the recipient, they may also result in political and military relationships that could be embarrassing to the supplier or lead to unwanted commitments in the region. Fourth, military assistance may enhance internal security, providing a measure of personal protection for the citizens of a recipient nation, but such assistance also may be used to repress them in the pursuit of democratic process or recourse to corruption.

A fifth point is that the stability that arms and assistance promote may lead to increased foreign investment and economic growth, but arms purchases and military expenditures are sizable diversions of both money and manpower from the civilian economy, thus retarding economic development. In addition, arms purchases on credit add to external foreign debt and annual debt-service payments, causing increased balance-of-payments and foreign-exchange problems. Sixth, since arms transfers and military assistance enhance the growth and modernization of local military forces, they contribute to national security and perceptions of sovereignty of recipient nations. But if the price of these weapons includes basing rights, agreements on prices of oil or other commodities, or political support in the United Nations or on sensitive issues such as South Africa, these may be viewed as net reductions in sovereignty and security, jealously guarded commodities in Africa and the rest of the Third World.

Seventh, arms sales represent for suppliers a means of easing their own balance-of-payments problems and contributing to the development of indigenous defense industries. Yet provision of state-of-the-art weapons may detract from their own military readiness and require the provision of substantial numbers of technicians and support to insure absorption of the weapons by recipients. Finally, since the Falklands crisis there is growing concern that the provision of arms to recipient nations that are neutral or friendly today—an enhancement of supplier political influence—raises the specter of having intervention forces countered by their own weapons. The converse of this for recipient nations is that use of transferred arms may be constrained by end-use agreements and embargoes that preclude resupply.

Recipient nations recognize that supplier nations are seeking political influence or leverage through the provision of arms and military assistance. As a result, recipients studiously avoid, whenever possible, situations in which they must become too closely linked with suppliers. The irony is, however, that they are in fact dependent upon one or another industrialized nations for arms, and thus are willing to grant (or begrudge) suppliers a degree of political influence.

Yet this situation is not so one-sided as it may seem and as others would like one to believe. Because alternative suppliers are competing with each other for political influence, African and other recipient nations are in a position to manipulate those who would influence or manipulate them. They can do so, for example, by granting military access rather than basing agreements, and then using one or another strategy to bargain for better terms in the future.[18]

One such strategy, perhaps the best in such a competitive environment, is simply to threaten to seek another supplier of weapons. The current supplier would be likely to interpret such a decision as a net loss in regional influence and thus be much more willing to provide arms or assistance on more favorable terms. In other words, it may be in the best interests of an African nation to allow itself to become "dependent" on an arms supplier and then radically shift its orientation (or at least threaten to do so).

By allowing a supplier nation considerable initial access at relatively little cost, permitting it the opportunity to invest heavily in facility development, and fostering a kind of strategic and operational dependency, a recipient nation may be able to have a much stronger subsequent bargaining position. Such developments may also permit the recipient nation to plead instability and the need for increased military aid or more concessionary terms to either placate critics or stifle opposition. By blaming economic problems on the presence of foreign troops from the supplier nation or on accompanying political discontent, a recipient nation may not cause withdrawal of troops but instead may enhance its position vis-à-vis the supplier that seeks to keep them there for larger strategic reasons.

In essence, many "mini-states" are coming to recognize their importance to the more powerful states, not only as support in the United Nations but also in pursuit of strategic goals.[19] In the short run, many of these states have more influence on the superpowers than is commonly believed. The fact is that military and economic interdependence has made the industrialized nations at least as dependent upon the Third World as the Third World is dependent upon them. In Africa, the United States and its allies are dependent upon the maintenance of political stability and the provision of strategic resources and military access. Even though African nations need to market their exports in the West, they do not need to provide U.S. or other military forces basing or access. In fact, such actions may be counterproductive, as accusations of neocolonialism heighten domestic political tensions and threaten political stability. As a result, most access agreements are predicated upon the ability of the recipient nation to selectively grant access on a case-by-case basis.

Thus military access in times of crisis will be determined by the international and domestic political situations of the granting nation. Just as many North Atlantic Treaty Organization (NATO) allies refused access and overflight privileges to U.S. aircraft resupplying the Israelis in 1967 and 1973, so too might African nations deny use of facilities because it might jeopardize their own interests.[20]

Military assistance is critical in this situation, not because it will necessarily permit the United States to threaten an African nation into compliance with its strategic access needs, but because decisions to grant access will be made only when the leaders of the nation in question are confident that their armed forces are capable of insuring the internal and external security of their own nation. Such favorable decisions therefore are dependent upon *prior* provision of sufficient military assistance by the United States and other nations. To say that the United States is "buying" access with arms is facile; what it is acquiring is a degree of stability that will permit recipient nations to grant access at a later time. Such stability is derived from the overall state of military development in the country—not just the provision of arms by the United States.

In fact, there is growing evidence that arms transfers *do not* provide suppliers the degree of leverage their supporters would like to believe.[21] The diversity of available suppliers limits their ability to threaten recipients with cutoffs, and the trend among developing nations has been to deal with several suppliers despite problems of standardization. Some African nations may have difficulty in attracting any arms suppliers, but those who do are besieged with opportunities to acquire arms.

A recent study conducted by the United States Army War College indicates that the environment of military or security assistance has changed drastically, that the concept of dealing only with friends and allies is outmoded, and that agreements based upon a narrow quid pro quo are too restrictive (and thus not very appealing to recipient nations).[22] What is required are broad bilateral relations with recipient nations, rather than those focused on individual leaders with only narrow political support. Events in Nicaragua, Iran, and elsewhere indicate the efficacy of such a new interpretation of the role of arms transfers and foreign policy. Or as one analyst has asked, "Who can say with any certainty to what extent a favourable political situation is due to military assistance?

How does one judge the ratio of military assistance to economic aid in a regime where power grows from the barrel of a gun?"[23]

Nor are such outcomes limited to the United States. As a recent congressional study summarized:

> The American experiences in Vietnam, Iran, and Ethiopia graphically illustrate that arms transfers, and even the use of American troops, do not ensure "stability" in a country or region, or guarantee the continued good will and cooperation of recipient nations. The Soviet Union has had similar setbacks in the use of arms sales as an instrument of foreign policy in nations such as Egypt, Somalia, and even a fellow Communist state, the People's Republic of China. In short, arms transfers are an unwieldy instrument of foreign policy and they do not always provide the results expected.[24]

Pull Factors and Recipient Considerations

Before examining the principal sources and scope of arms transfers to Africa, it will be useful to examine in some detail the factors that contribute to the demand for arms. Although these factors are essentially political in nature and have been discussed in some detail in the preceding chapter, their specific effect on arms transfers will be examined here.

Despite evidence that the suppliers of arms are quite aggressive in their pursuit of customers, directly or indirectly encouraged by their own nation's pursuit of foreign-policy objectives, research into "who is supplying what to whom" indicates that the single most important factor in the trade in arms with Africa has been the demand for arms by African nations.[25] Characterized as *pull factors*, both the increase in intra-African conflict and the expanding African resource base have contributed to the overall growth in the supply of arms to the region.

Although "the increase in Africa's arms imports is caused by the conflict behavior of many African nations, including various internal conflicts,"[26] many question that this in fact is the result of African preferences and interests. As indicated in Chapter 1, many firmly believe that supplier nations are somehow forcing arms on Africans instead of giving them economic assistance. This hypothesis is contrary to the reality of the drive for military development within Africa. As one U.S. official has said, "We gave them $50 million in PL-480 (food) assistance in fiscal '79. Of course, they would have preferred weapons."[27]

Much of the conflict in contemporary Africa may be attributed to the failure of the Organization of African Unity and African solidarity to overcome interstate competition and rivalry, the resurgence of tribal and ethnic factors, the instability wrought by military intervention in domestic politics, and the failure of many African nations to achieve sufficient economic progress. In addition, these essentially internal factors have been supplemented by irredentist movements, expansionist nationalism, foreign intervention, and transborder military intervention by neighboring states.[28] Although internal, domestic issues and conflict remain unresolved, it is clear that the increased demand for arms is more a response to other external threats than a solution to internal discord.[29]

In peacetime, or in the absence of viable threats to the security of African nations, the military plays a special role in reinforcing popular perceptions of independence and sovereignty. As Pres. Hamani Diori stated at the inauguration of the new army of Niger, "Henceforth, in the eyes of the world and of the whole of our people, you are the visible sign of our political independence and of our proclaimed will to defend it against all aggression."[30] These sentiments are shared by all African leaders regardless of ideological orientation—military power is seen as a prerequisite of sovereignty. And in a region so recently freed from colonial rule, the costs associated with creating and maintaining such power are insignificant compared with the benefits of independence.

The symbolic value of weapons will be dealt with in more detail in the following chapter. However, it has particular relevance in explaining why there has been an increased demand not only for arms but also for the most sophisticated military technology available. There is little interest on the part of African leaders in what they perceive as surplus, obsolete, export-only, "junk weapons,"[31] and most African nations are in the market for weapons that will modernize their forces with a state-of-the-art capability serviceable into the 1990s and beyond.[32] This desire has manifested itself not only in advanced Western systems such as the Jaguar and F14 fighter aircraft,[33] but in Western-produced systems in general, which are commonly perceived as being technologically superior to those provided (although at much lower cost) by the Soviets and other communist nations. As one Chadian official has said, "We accept Russian weapons because we have nothing else. But we would much rather have American made weapons if we could get them."[34]

Many African nations have a number of arms suppliers, for the reasons outlined above, and both the security and symbolic aspects of arms-transfer relationships can militate against a supplier's developing much regional influence. The simple fact is that given the large number of African nations, their changing and diverse national interests, and the dynamics of interstate relations, a supplier may easily find itself providing arms to both sides of a long-standing dispute. This is what happened to the Soviets with Libya and Egypt and with Somalia and Ethiopia. Often in its pursuit of military access in the region, the United States fails to see African security concerns in regional terms, wherein African neighbors—rather than the Soviets—pose the most significant threat. A good example of this was recent Kenyan dissatisfaction with U.S. supplies of air defense weapons to the Somalis. As one Kenyan official put it, "You supply us with planes and the Somalis with equipment to shoot them down."[35]

Another factor that concerns recipients is the speed at which the arms are delivered. African threat perceptions more often than not are immediate, and the responsiveness of suppliers may be more important than the quality of the weapons or even the terms of their sale.[36] Delivery problems are often seen as deliberate slowdowns for arms control considerations and irritate African leaders, who see how responsive suppliers can be if their own interests are threatened or if the recipient has more importance to the supplier.[37] Conditions imposed by suppliers through end-use agreements and enforced through "spare parts diplomacy"[38] only serve to reinforce perceptions that the purpose of arms transfers is not a genuine concern on the part of suppliers for recipients' needs, but rather achievement of suppliers' foreign-policy goals.

A final consideration in selecting suppliers of military equipment is their overall responsiveness to the needs of the recipient. This goes beyond the speed of delivery or the willingness to provide state-of-the-art equipment and instead deals with issues involving the long-term effects of arms transfers on the recipient and the personal relationships established among personnel from both countries. These issues constitute the core of a supplier country's "style" and very often have more impact on the quality of the interstate relationship than the equipment itself. In short, there is a premium attached to relationships that seem to the participants to be less paternalistic and more egalitarian and that appear to make enduring contributions to the military self-reliance of the recipient nations.

Push Factors and Supplier Styles

Even though arms transfers and military assistance may not be the most effective instrument of foreign policy and may tend to be somewhat unwieldy and unreliable in their outcomes, it is unlikely that the supplier nations will forgo the opportunity to influence African states by voluntarily or unilaterally restraining their transfers of arms in response to African demands. But physical and fiscal limits to the amount and type of arms that may be supplied are imposed by other strategic considerations and the military and financial ability of individual suppliers to meet specific demands. Furthermore, one must recognize that when suppliers measure the costs and assumed benefits of arms transfers and military aid to African nations, the calculations are inherently subjective in nature: The effectiveness of arms transfers in furthering foreign-policy goals is at best uncertain, especially in determining to what extent a favorable outcome is in fact due to military assistance. As one official put it: "I would submit that there is no way of assuring stability, supporting friendly regimes, or irrevocably winning the support of the military in Africa, let alone making formidable fighting machines out of armies."[39]

Before surveying the characteristics of the major and secondary suppliers of arms to Africa, it is important to note that the data are imperfect in both quantitative and qualitative terms. Comparing Soviet, U.S., and other arms transfers provides at best only a suggestion of the direction and scope of the trade and supply of arms and military assistance. Statistics compiled by suppliers and recipients are notoriously inaccurate because of imperfections in currency valuations, calculations of what is military and what is nonmilitary in each budget or outlay, differing methods of national accounting, and concerns for secrecy.[40] Finally, there is the problem of determining the relative combat values of different systems, especially where it appears a country is spending more to procure fewer systems.[41]

Given these limitations, the analysis of arms transfers becomes more of an intuitive process. Therefore the following descriptions of individual suppliers to Africa will focus on qualitative issues regarding supplier motivations, recipient responses, and an overall assessment of the "styles" of arms-transfer behavior. For more detailed analyses of the quantitative aspects of arms transfers to individual countries, more statistically oriented studies are available elsewhere.[42]

Eastern-Bloc Arms Transfers

The Soviet Union and its Warsaw Pact allies are the principal suppliers of arms and military assistance in Africa. The Soviets alone are responsible for over half of the dollar value of arms transferred to the region and for over three-fourths of the number of systems transferred. This trend is likely to continue throughout the 1980s. (See Tables 4 and 5, Statistical Appendix.)

Not the least of the reasons for this trend is the Soviets' continuing competition with the United States for influence in Africa and with the People's Republic of China for ideological leadership in Africa as a quasi-socialist, nonaligned, and anticolonial region.[43] But the Soviet dominance of the arms trade in Africa stems from even deeper issues that have caused military assistance to become the principal form of

Soviet aid to Africa. Put succinctly, Soviet economic and technical aid has been a virtual failure in the region, whereas its military ventures have enjoyed a modicum of success.[44]

There are a number of reasons for this. First, the Soviets enjoy very little credibility as providers of sound economic advice.[45] In a recent article, Anatoly Gromyko suggested that African nations should reorient their economies to agriculture and curtail mining and other industrialization programs.[46] While this might be wise advice, his suggestion that they do so with Soviet, not Western, expertise ignored the dismal performance of Soviet agriculture.

Second, the West has frequently denied military aid requested by African nations, and the Soviets have been quick to fill such orders.[47] Soviet arms cost 50 percent less, are delivered 50 percent faster, and are significantly less complex than their Western counterparts.[48] The continuing willingness of the Soviets to supply expensive, increasingly advanced weapons systems on short notice,[49] together with their large stocks of surplus equipment and longer production lines,[50] has made them more responsive to the security needs of many African countries. In addition, continued Soviet willingness to transfer arms on a grant-aid basis, to sell them at extremely concessionary rates and terms, and to accept payment in local currencies or commodities has made Soviet arms even more attractive to African nations with weak economies and severe balance-of-payments problems.[51]

A further dimension is the Soviet willingness to provide arms to African nations during conflict and to national liberation movements. Their supplying of MIGs to Nigeria during its civil war is more a reflection of Soviet opportunism than commitment to any political principle, and their continued ability to supply large quantities of major equipment to revolutionary groups insures their influence with the new governments once they are established. This latter trend is especially significant, since many African governments that approach the West for military aid are confronted not with a handful of lightly armed insurgents, but rather with large, well-organized armies, equipped with increasingly sophisticated weapons.[52]

But despite the very great African demand for military aid and the Soviet willingness and ability to supply it, there are significant limitations on the amount of influence that aid provides the Soviets in the region. Much of this can be attributed to Soviet ineptitude and what has come to be known as "the ugly Russian problem."[53] Gerald Bender has observed that "the very style that earned U.S. citizens the reputation of 'ugly Americans' in the 1950s and 1960s appears to characterize the Soviets in the 1970s. Throughout the continent, Africans complain that the Soviets are clannish, impatient, and that they treat them like difficult children."[54]

In addition to this cultural insensitivity, much of which may be attributed to the prejudiced nature of Soviet society as a whole, the Russians have not always dealt fairly with their arms-transfer partners with regard to economic issues. Because of Angolan dependence upon the Soviets and their allies for military aid, the Soviets have been able to renege on several promises of economic assistance and technical aid. In addition, Russian fishing fleets have been depleting Angolan waters.[55] Furthermore, since the Soviets are willing to accept payment in commodities, yet are short of hard currency themselves, they are frequently tempted to dump commodities on the world market rather than import them for domestic consumption. They did this with Ethiopian coffee in the late 1970s, with negative consequences for both the Ethiopian economy and Soviet influence in the Horn of Africa.[56]

Eastern-bloc military aid itself is, while plentiful, poor in quality and in the way it is delivered. Furthermore, although the arms themselves are not always very sophisticated or very well made (not necessarily disadvantages for technology absorption, but certainly for prestige purposes—see the next two chapters), the Soviets retain close control of arms through spare-parts diplomacy and through the requirement of a large number of Eastern-bloc technicians to operate and maintain weapons.

This manifests itself in several ways. For one thing, the training given to Africans both at home and in the Soviet Union is of insufficient quality and duration. Whereas "the acceptance of military personnel for training at Soviet military installations and the dispatch of large numbers of Soviet military technicians to less developed countries subsequently have proved to be important elements of the Soviet military assistance program,"[57] the training Africans and others from the Third World receive cannot compare to that offered in the West. For example, in a recent analysis of the Iran-Iraq war several lessons emerged:

> The first is that, at least to date, the USSR has done a miserable job of training and equipping developing nations with SAM and fighter defenses. The few air forces that have had any success with Soviet equipment— Egypt and India—have had this success largely because they rejected Soviet tactics and bought outside technical advice and supporting equipment. It is, of course, impossible to know just how much different Soviet training and equipment is in its "export" version, but it is clear that numbers can largely be discounted when a developing country relies on Soviet equipment and advice. . . . One senior Arab military officer, who had been consulted on Iraq's problems, said that he found the Soviet

training course given to Iraq's pilots had been far too short and very undemanding. . . . His private reaction was that neither the training in the USSR, nor the advice on training in Iraq served the Iraqis well. . . .[58]

Such inadequacies extend to logistics and maintenance as well. "The Nigerian Air force has suffered from poor maintenance of its existing jet aircraft as well as Soviet reluctance in supplying spare parts."[59] Egyptian, Somalian, and Sudanese alienation by Soviet tightfistedness in both training and maintenance contributed to their ejection of the Soviets in the late 1970s. It appears that the same characteristic may cause even the Ethiopians to do the same. "Some Ethiopians say Moscow is unwilling to pass on technology, citing the fact that the jet engines on Ethiopia's Soviet-built fighter planes and helicopters must be sent back to the Soviet Union for servicing. Ethiopian mechanics are capable of doing the work since they serviced the military's American-built F5 jet fighters, and Ethiopian Airlines does all its own maintenance."[60]

This reluctance on the part of the Soviets to transfer technology is manifested throughout the Third World. It would be more appropriate to describe the Soviets as providing equipment rather than as rendering assistance in the process of military development. Two recent studies indicate that while the United States and its allies provide twice as much training and support as they do weapons (in dollar amounts), the Soviets devote 70 to 80 percent of their military assistance to weapons.[61] Clearly, if the goal of arms purchases is to develop a degree of military self-reliance that has potential spin-offs to the civilian economy, Western sources would be preferable.

Soviet Surrogates

Given the inadequacy of training by the Soviets and their refusal to transfer technology to Africans in a way that would further their military development, it is not surprising that the Soviets have found themselves relying to a great extent upon their allies or surrogates to operate and maintain transferred equipment. Soviet pilots have been reported flying MIGs in Angola and Mozambique,[62] and Cubans, East Germans, and others have been actively engaged in military operations in Africa.[63] Much of this may be the result of Soviet failure to anticipate the longer training periods required for Third World pilots generally,[64] causing the Soviets to provide trained personnel as a stopgap measure. But what is more likely is the growing African disenchantment with the "ugly Russian" described above. As one Angolan official put it, "When the Soviets arrive here, they usually demand rooms in the best hotels or well-furnished houses with air conditioning and new stoves and re-frigerators, which costs us a lot of our precious foreign exchange—

whereas we can put five or six Cubans in a hot one-bedroom apartment with mattresses on the floor and we will never hear a complaint."[65]

But even if the Cubans do not alienate the Africans with whom they come in contact, they can wear out their welcome. Many Angolans are beginning to question the value of a sizable Cuban troop presence in their country that does not seem to be deployed to fight or even to deter South African incursions. Instead the Cubans are used to protect Gulf Oil installations and party leaders and to pacify internal political opposition, all at great expense to the Angolans.[66]

Frustration with the Soviets and their allies has even caused the Angolans to consider new economic ties with Portugal. Although such a rapid rapprochement with Angola's former colonial power may shock outsiders, the need for more effective economic assistance compels the Angolans. Although they will most likely continue their Eastern-bloc military ties, the inadequacies of Soviet economic aid are quite apparent to them and have prompted a general turning to the West.[67]

This reorientation on the part of African leaders marks the continued decline of Soviet influence in the region. Since the Soviets and their allies essentially can render only military aid to countries in desperate need of economic assistance, and since Africans recognize that, as one official put it, "you can't eat guns,"[68] this trend is likely to continue. This does not mean that the Soviets will cease to be a significant factor in Africa—at least until the problems of South Africa are resolved, but it does mean that a policy of arms over economics is likely to fail. The Soviets do appear to be changing their strategy somewhat and to be offering more economic pledges in lieu of military aid,[69] but their ability to compete in this arena is severely constrained.

This situation is further exacerbated by the fact that the reputation of Soviet arms as "simple, rugged, and reliable"[70] may work against them as African nations seek to modernize their armed forces with state-of-the-art equipment and to pursue a course of military development. In addition, competition within the Eastern bloc for ideological leadership further erodes the ability of the Soviets to use arms as an instrument of policy. Even the closest Soviet allies in the region—the East Europeans and the Cubans—are not mere puppets of the Soviet policy. Each appears to pursue, within limitations, its own economic and political goals in the region.[71]

China and North Korea

The competition within the Eastern bloc is especially evident in Zimbabwe, where both the North Koreans and the Chinese have been actively providing alternative military aid to the Mugabe government. The Chinese, long a "marginal but steady supplier" of arms to Tanzania,

Congo, Zaire, and Guinea,[72] have recently agreed to provide twenty-five MIG25s and pilot and ground crew training to replace white pilots and aircraft lost since independence.[73] The North Koreans have been present in Zimbabwe since 1981, arming and training a "Fifth Brigade" that is loyal to Mugabe and likely to be employed against his political enemies.[74] Their failure in Zaire in the mid-1970s, where the troops they trained were reported to be some of the worst in the country, may be repeated. Recent reports indicate that the unit in Zimbabwe has been on a rampage in southern Zimbabwe, indiscriminately killing, raping, and looting.[75]

It is fairly evident that Chinese military activities in the region are designed to directly compete with the Soviets. Such is not the case with the North Koreans. Although their activities in Zaire were apparently at the behest of the Soviet Union, it seems that Zimbabwean reluctance to deal with the Soviets (who backed the Nkomo faction that opposed Mugabe during the recent war) would preclude the North Koreans' acting as a Soviet surrogate. What is more likely is that the North Koreans see this as an opportunity to gain greater recognition vis-à-vis the South Koreans and to reinstate their somewhat tarnished nonaligned credentials.

Western-Bloc Arms Transfers

Arms provided to Africa by Western suppliers differ significantly from those of the Eastern bloc. First, despite the U.S. role as leading supplier in the West, the market is competitive, rather than cooperative as in the East. Second, although arms are transferred for policy reasons, their economic importance to Western suppliers is much greater. Third, like Western technology generally, U.S., French, and other arms are much more sophisticated than their Soviet or other counterparts. Fourth, unlike the Soviet and Warsaw Pact nations, the Western countries lack large quantities of surplus weapons that can be rapidly transferred to recipients on a grant-aid or concessionary credit basis. Instead, they must manufacture and sell arms on credit, subject to the dynamics of their own and the recipients' economies. Finally, the Western nations are democracies, and although they may exercise some discretion in publicizing their arms transfers, their policies and partners are often the subject of public debate and likely to change as governments change.

France

The French are the major Western supplier of arms to Africa. This reflects the lack of U.S. interest in the region (at least until recently) as much as it does the continued importance of the region to France. The numerous military aid and access agreements that France has maintained since African independence were brought into being to resolve the contradiction between continuing French economic and security interests in its former colonies and the desire for African nationalism and independence.[76] By pursuing a policy limited to traditional areas of interest and employing a variety of means of involvement on a case-by-case basis,[77] the French have largely been able to avoid accusations of neocolonialism and have earned the appreciation of their African allies.[78]

French arms transfers have important domestic economic consequences and also play a critical part in what France sees as its "proper political role" between the superpowers.[79] By maintaining an impressive military and technical presence in Africa, the French are able to pursue a foreign policy independent of the United States and thus offer African nations both an economic and political alternative that fits with a policy of nonalignment. Despite frequent cooperation with Americans during some of France's intervention operations in Zaire, Chad, and elsewhere, the French have been careful to disassociate themselves from U.S. policy (especially toward South Africa) and to play down their perceived role as the "gendarme of Africa."[80]

The recent decision by the Mitterrand government to reaffirm its African ties[81] was marked by the subtle change of designating its forces based in the region as *force d'assistance* rather than *force d'intervention*. Although the French are outnumbered by Soviet and Cuban forces, they are better organized and distributed in the region and, taken together with the twenty-two thousand *cooperants* (technical assistance personnel), they have the potential to effectively influence or intervene in affairs throughout the region.[82]

Arms transfers are an important means of exercising this influence. Just as Mitterrand was forced by realities to reconsider the Socialist position advocating a French military withdrawal from Africa, so too was he compelled by both foreign policy concerns and domestic employment issues to continue the arms-transfer policies of previous governments. Although he advocated a policy of "less arms, more machine tools," the fact that the French arms industry is dependent upon exports and that many of his own party's members worked in its factories have insured that the arms business would be as usual.[83]

There are indications that the French will in fact be expanding their share of the African market, selling to nations not normally considered their customers, on a credit basis.[84] And despite the continuing debate in France and within the Socialist party regarding arms sales, the commercial basis of such transfers is likely to continue. As one official recently said, "We are merchants. If the clients want to announce a sale or not, that's their business. We never say anything—it's our golden rule. We leave the client free to do whatever he wants."[85]

West Germany

West Germany's role as a major supplier of arms to Africa also has been subjected to scrutiny. Although it was one of the first postindependence suppliers to the region, in 1978 disclosures of West Germany's arms transfers to South Africa, Rhodesia, and both sides in the Nigerian civil war caused a public uproar.[86] Despite its stated policy of not transferring arms to areas of tension West Germany, like France, finds it needs arms exports to support its defense industries and rearmament programs. This has subjected the government to criticisms of hypocrisy not unlike those in France. Hans Dieter Genscher said in 1980, "We cannot afford to look on idly while arms are pumped into developing countries that need not guns but schools and hospitals, tractors and lathes."[87] Yet the transfers continue, outranking even those of the United States in Africa. West Germany has even constructed small-arms factories in Guinea, Nigeria, and Sudan.[88]

Great Britain

The British continue to offer arms and assistance to their former colonies in Africa, though clearly for economic rather than for political goals. In order to support its own military modernization, the United Kingdom needs arms sales to create economies of scale and to sustain employment in its defense industries. Policy motives are claimed only after the fact.[89] Although at first it appeared that the Thatcher government would be trimming defense, in the aftermath of the Falklands war it appears that many of the proposed cuts in the navy will be restored.[90] Perhaps more important than arms themselves are the military aid and advice that British officers and technicians are rendering in Africa.[91] Another outgrowth of the Falklands crisis that has further enhanced the British position in the region was the refusal of Great Britain to accept South African offers of access to Simonstown, an issue that caused considerable controversy in the early 1970s.[92]

Other Suppliers

In a similar vein, other Westen suppliers find themselves caught between contradictory pressures to cease being "merchants of death" and at the same time to maintain high levels of employment and independent arms industries.[93] Forced to seek Third World markets because of the increasing U.S. arms imports to NATO, Western nations' arms industries are thriving as African and other nations seek arms without political strings. The Belgians,[94] Italians,[95] Austrians,[96] and

Canadians[97] all are extremely active as arms suppliers in Africa. Given the world economic recession and the needs of these countries to maximize exports of all kinds, it is unlikely that their arms sales will diminish over the next decade.

The United States

U.S. arms transfers are also unlikely to be reduced, because of a renewed policy emphasizing security assistance and because of the increased African demand for arms of a more sophisticated nature. After Vietnam, military assistance was seen by both the U.S. public and Congress as a bankrupt policy. In addition to shortages of surplus equipment to transfer to African countries on a grant-aid basis (much of it was left in Vietnam, only to be retransferred elsewhere by the Vietnamese), the Military Assistance Program was curtailed and Foreign Military Sales became the dominant means of U.S. arms transfers.

With the advent of the Carter administration, a new policy viewing arms transfers as an *exceptional* instrument of influence was promulgated[98] and almost immediately was subject to harsh criticism from a variety of sources for limiting U.S. sales abroad and for failing to go far enough in doing so. Despite its policy of restraint, the administration "elected to use arms sales as a major weapon to challenge Soviet intrusion and influence into Africa."[99]

The Reagan administration has chosen to emphasize arms transfers as an important policy tool,[100] and it too has been subjected to equally harsh criticism for pushing arms sales and for undermining U.S. readiness by transferring arms that were needed by U.S. armed forces. An example of this criticism is a statement by Sen. William Proxmire: "The foreign policy of the United States under the Reagan administration more than any other administration in American history, is based on a single strategic factor—arms sales. We now sell arms to anyone, anywhere, for any reason. Arms sales have become a substitute for diplomatic effort, for arms control and for economic development."[101]

The administration has increased security assistance to Africa to gain military access to the region, to deter internal and external threats to African states, to promote economic development through political stability, and to reduce the likelihood of U.S. intervention in the region. As one administration official put it, "A little assistance buys a lot of security."[102] Security assistance can be interpreted as "buying" access for the Rapid Deployment Force and also as helping recipient nations to meet their perceived defense needs "by providing them the weapons they need to insure their security and training their personnel to operate and maintain those weapons."[103] Some regional leaders have even gone so far as to suggest that security assistance will permit U.S. forces to forward deploy equipment for later contingency use and that such a program would be mutually beneficial.[104]

At issue is not whether this policy represents a fundamental shift in U.S. orientation to Africa. Security assistance has always been a part of U.S. aid, and foreign-policy concerns have dictated the amounts and distribution of it.[105] Economic and military aid continue in balance, and as one observer noted, "While the United States has not responded adequately to Africa's pressing developmental needs, it has exercised some restraint in dispensing military largesse."[106] What is at issue is the appropriateness of military aid, regardless of amount, for meeting Africa's long-term security needs. As one Sudanese official put it, "We do not need arms from America. We need roads and economic help. That is much more important."[107]

Third World Suppliers

Arms exports to Africa and the developing world generally can be expected to increase over the next decade, and much of this growth will be attributed to the expanding markets of a new set of suppliers, the Newly Industrialized Countries (NICs). They will be seeking stronger ties with the nonaligned world, markets for fledgling armaments industries, improved balance of payments and, of course, political influence. Their ranks include such nations as Brazil, Argentina, South Africa, Israel, India, Yugoslavia, North and South Korea, and Taiwan.[108] They also include some unlikely candidates that lack sizable defense industries but possess a surplus of weapons (Egypt) or of trained manpower (Pakistan) and are likely to provide them as military assistance or as arms retransfers to African countries.[109]

Brazil

Brazil is an excellent example of an NIC that is penetrating the African arms market. Not only is Brazilian equipment "light, robust and simple," but Brazilians are sensitive to the perceptions of the recipients. As a Brazilian defense industry official states, "Our people get along better because we don't expect too much. We mix with them, drink their water, eat their food. They (the Soviets) keep to themselves and even import Russian water. Local people don't like that."[110] Through development of their own defense industrial base, Brazilians seem to combine the best of the French and Russian approaches to arms transfers—easily absorbed equipment with few questions asked. The absence of political strings, the fact that Brazil is nonaligned, and the apparent willingness to transfer technology all contribute to making Brazil one of the top ten arms suppliers (over $1 billion annually).[111] It must export arms to use its excess defense capacity and to aid its own balance-of-payments problems.[112]

South Africa

South Africa is the only significant arms producer in the region and possesses the potential and need to export arms as well. Its defense industries do not currently provide arms to other African states, although there are unconfirmed reports of its supplying arms to Morocco and to insurgents in Mozambique.[113] Much of its industry was developed through French and Israeli assistance, in violation or circumvention of the United Nations embargo. It is ironic that the Israelis, one of the primary sources of military and technical aid and advice to African countries in the early 1960s, have been caused by growing Afro-Arab solidarity to become more closely allied with South Africa, another "pariah" state.[114] This trend has only recently been reversed by recognition by Zaire and the conclusion of a military aid agreement between the two countries.[115]

Several African nations—in particular Nigeria—seek to create their own indigenous arms industries.[116] There are several reasons for this trend, not the least important of which is the symbolic value of such a capacity for national prestige and for deterring enemies. Not only do these industries lessen dependence upon external suppliers and the impact of spare-parts diplomacy (especially in light of the embargo placed on Argentina during the Falklands war), but they are tangible evidence of sovereignty and the ability of a nation to pursue its own course in foreign affairs.[117]

For most Africans, the most compelling motive for such a development has been the growing South African military-industrial complex that has effectively insulated them against arms embargoes.[118] Yet an attempt to develop such a complex merely to "keep up with the Afrikaners" would require even more military and financial assistance in the form of loans, technology transfer, licensing, and coproduction agreements and a further diversion of financial and human resources from economic development. This continued dependency, in one form or another, will continue to determine the patterns of conventional arms transfers to Africa. Since African nations perceive the need for arms and therefore demand them, yet cannot produce them or purchase them on a cash basis, they will be forced to concede political influence for arms. Although they might prefer to deal with the nonaligned producers such as Brazil, they will most likely be forced to continue to seek arms where credit is available.

Conclusions

In order to draw much of the above information together and to set the stage for discussions in subsequent chapters, it is useful to return to the issues cited earlier in this chapter concerning the precolonial arms trade with Africa. Not a great deal has changed, despite the colonial interlude:

- The terms of trade remain unfavorable to African nations. Despite concessionary credit and grant-aid programs, when African nations seek armaments, they must do so in a market dominated by the industrialized nations. Although the terms of credit or purchase may not be as financially demanding as a cash-and-carry transaction, the political costs associated with such transfers can be enormous.
- The weapons themselves, though not necessarily of inferior quality, are usually inappropriate for the environment and absorptive capacity of recipient nations. To maintain and operate them, African nations must accept an influx of foreign technicians whose presence increases rather than reduces African dependency upon the supplier country.
- Because of the desire to preserve their independence and some semblance of nonalignment, African nations continue to have a diversity of weapons in their arsenals, exacerbating supply and maintenance problems.
- The shortage of skilled personnel and adequate facilities, chronic throughout all sectors of African nations, persists and may detract from other programs as these resources are drained away to meet military requirements.
- There is a lack of training because of its expense, the infrastructure needed to perform it, and the tendency of all governments to cut operations and maintenance budgets during lean years. As a result, equipment is damaged by inexperienced personnel, thus losing its deterrent and defense capability and requiring even more external support, or replacement.

Recognizing that these conditions persist is one thing; doing something to correct them is another. As will be seen in the following chapters, the political economy of defense and the crucial role of manpower resources in defense are part of larger issues. The process of military development cannot be divorced from the overall processes of economic growth and political modernization. The part that arms transfers play in meeting, at least in the immediate future, the security needs of African nations cannot be considered separately from either growth or modernization, as they are critical elements of the environment in which military development occurs. The demand for arms is motivated by the difficulties Africans are experiencing with these phenomena. Although many African leaders are proving quite adept at manipulating many of the suppliers of arms, that in itself will not change the fundamental nature of the arms-transfer relationship unless Africans take action either to reduce their need for security or to seek alternative forms of military development.

The Political Economy
of New Conventional Weapons

In a civilized society, as the soldiers are maintained altogether by the labour of those who are not soldiers, the number of the former can never exceed what the latter can maintain.

—Adam Smith
The Wealth of Nations, Vol. 2, p. 190

As indicated in Chapter 3, the transfer of arms to Africa has increased dramatically in the preceding decade, in both quantitative and qualitative terms. Much of the latter increase is due to the increasing demand for, and supply of, "new conventional weapons," or precision-guided munitions.[1] It is true that the introduction of these more powerful, highly sophisticated weapons systems has implications for both the arms control and security policies of supplier nations, but these weapons have an even more critical impact on the defense policies and capabilities of recipient nations.

The ability of African nations to absorb these new systems will be analyzed in more detail in the following chapter. Here I would like to introduce the possibility that they have in fact been oversold in terms of their cost effectiveness, their true military capabilities, and their ultimate contribution to the security and stability of the regimes that procure them. The reality is that these new conventional weapons, rather than contributing to the defense of the recipients, may in fact be internally destabilizing and may contribute to the overall level and intensity of conflict in the region. Despite claims that these weapons will "revolutionize warfare,"[2] even the industrialized nations are experiencing difficulties in acquiring and absorbing them. As one commentator noted, "The new weapons are so costly we have to reduce the numbers we can acquire, and they are so complex that they are difficult to keep battle-ready. We face the staggering prospect of decreasing our preparedness as we increase our budget."[3]

The focus of this chapter is the political economy of new conventional weapons in Africa. By *political economy* I mean the fundamental relationship between resource allocation and the distribution of power or influence within the nation-state.[4] In this chapter I will examine the factors that influence African leaders to demand new conventional weapons, the effects that such decisions have on their overall economy, and internal and external political relations.

Global Versus Grass-Roots Analysis

Before doing this, however, it is necessary to discuss one of the most difficult problems confronting those who make arms-transfers decisions—the dichotomy between global and grass-roots levels of analysis. On the global level, arms transfers are a commonly used instrument of supplier nation foreign policy. It is vital here to emphasize that transfer decisions are made on the basis of supplier interests, without regard to the impact they will have on the recipient, except as it may influence the goals of the supplier. It is precisely at this—the grass-roots level—that so many supplier intentions and interests go awry.

It is not that the representatives of supplier nations located in recipient countries are ignorant of factors such as technology absorption, but rather that recipient interests simply take lower priority than those of the suppliers. This is not to advocate that supplier nations suddenly become charitable institutions (would that such were possible). But too often short-term global policies are implemented without reference to their regional or local long-term impact, and the results are in fact counterproductive for both parties to the exchange.

A similar situation obtains for recipient-nation leaders as well. Pull factors—the reasons why African nations demand arms—are exceptionally intense. It is in the nature of the regimes of the developing world that these more immediate considerations take priority over more long-term issues simply because their leaders perceive that investments in the future are no guarantee of staying in office and are therefore inclined to ignore grass-roots issues no matter how glaring or relevant they may be. Put another way, many African leaders are interested in regime survival rather than state enhancement, and problems that can only be anticipated pale in significance when compared to the tangible, pressing demands of the present.

Certainly this perpetual state of crisis management is nothing new in Africa and may be found elsewhere in virtually all governments. Nevertheless the growing and competing demands for resources that are of increasing scarcity in the region intensify the urgency with which security and defense decisions are made. Both arms suppliers and recipients make transfer decisions in response to immediate perceptions of threats and interests, and bureaucratic time-horizons—never noted for their breadth anywhere—shrink in scope as African governments endure or fall within a few hours or days of instability and violence.

In such an environment, supplier nations are compelled to respond to recipient requests for support, recognition, and assistance, *even when deliveries of military assistance may not be made for months or years.* It is little wonder that such decisions are often taken without regard to grass-roots considerations of the long-term effects they may have. What is even more important is that once such decisions have been made, they become part of the institutionalized relationship between supplier and recipient, even when the need for such transfers has evaporated. Thus arms-transfer agreements, often negotiated and decided in the heat of the moment, create important global linkages between participants that more often than not are more important than their content.

Another dimension of this dichotomy pertains directly to misapprehensions concerning arms transfers and arms races. Much of the analytical literature contends that arms transfers *cause* conflict.[5] But such concerns are misplaced: Even though more arms, especially those of a more advanced design, might cause a political rival to seek his own symbolic deterrent to the perceived threat such weapons create, the decision to fight or not most likely has already been made—in some cases centuries before. Military superiority, or relative inferiority, may influence *when* combat might take place, but to blame arms alone is to ignore the fact that deep-rooted ethnic, tribal, and other enmities have persisted regardless of what arms have been transferred.[6] Again, it is an issue of perspective, since

> from a *global* perspective, an increasing arms trade, consisting of more and more sophisticated weapons, is potentially more likely to lead to war and insecurity than a decreasing arms trade. But from a *national* perspective, in which each country evaluates its own interests, a decrease in a nation's arms procurement may not appear attractive, particularly if its neighbors are increasing their arsenals. On the contrary, a nation may feel that its security will be enhanced by purchasing more arms. (emphasis in original)[7]

In addition to the issue of arms control—that arms transfers fuel regional conflicts—there is growing concern that weapons sold to Third World countries may be used subsequently against the supplier or its allies. Again, the Falklands war is a vivid example of this. Many of the arms used by the Argentines were of British, U.S., or European manufacture. Even though those same allies imposed a temporary arms embargo against Argentina (as much because of their determination that

Argentina was an aggressor as out of concern for British feelings), it did not remove the element of irony that so many British casualties were the result of arms of their own manufacture. The same applies in Africa, for all of the major suppliers who have organized or already deployed intervention forces in the region. Would it be any more acceptable to Americans to sustain losses caused by weapons of Soviet, rather than U.S. manufacture?

Political Issues

There are a number of reasons for the increasing demand for arms by nations of the Third World, but many of them are fundamentally misunderstood by the industrialized supplier nations. Much of this misunderstanding may be attributed to the industrialized countries' being, for the most part, at a very different stage of their political evolution than their developing counterparts. Many of the things we take for granted are seen by developing nations as very fragile, valuable commodities, recently won through independence. Thus, their priorities are very different from ours, even though our goals ultimately may be similar.

Unless these differences are understood, arms transfers to developing nations will make very little sense. And since these transfers have come to be a vital instrument of foreign policy, they must be conducted intelligently in order to maximize their effectiveness and prevent their causing the opposite outcomes to those intended.

Sovereignty and Security

Although it may seem somewhat commonplace, it is useful to note that since the time of Adam Smith the sovereignty of the nation-state has been considered congruent with the security (both physical and symbolic) of that political entity. Even though the industrialized nations place great importance on security concerns (as evidenced by their military expenditures), sovereignty itself is more or less taken for granted. Although the recent Falklands crisis may be considered a conflict arising from sovereignty issues, ultimately there was no question that either party to the conflict was threatened in its very existence as an independent nation-state.

Such considerations are radically different, however, for the newly independent nations of the Third World. For them, their recently won sovereignty could just as easily be taken away—by a superpower, a former colonial power, or one of several emerging regional powers with historical or irredentist claims upon its territories or peoples. Again, using the Falklands as an example, the crisis arose differently for the

British and the Argentines: For the former, claims upon the islands were a challenge to its status as a major power; for the latter, the islands were a symbolic vestige of neocolonialism and a means of asserting and reinforcing its sovereignty and status as an emerging regional power. There was no question on either side that Britain and Argentina would endure as nations; but there was great doubt and speculation that either or both *governments* would survive the crisis. In the end, the Thatcher government was successful and the Galtieri regime fell. Again, this is another factor of great significance to developing nations—the fragility of existing political leadership and the process of its change. While British loss of the Falklands might have caused the Thatcher government to fall, it certainly would not have created a political crisis comparable to that experienced in Argentina after its defeat.

Many Third World leaders, having brought their countries to independence, *are* the nation. Their downfall would threaten both the sovereignty and the existence of the state, and therefore loss of more symbolic than essential elements of independence may bring about chaos and the disintegration of the nation.

Defense and Development

Preventing this chaos demands expenditures for defense. In the industrialized countries, debates concerning guns and butter create a great deal of political friction. Such debates are even more heated for developing nations because of the constrained resources base from which defense expenditures must come.

Most definitions of national security include two elements: The first concerns the physical protection of a territory and its population; the second recognizes the importance of the broad economic base that underlies the existence of the state, thus making defense of its territory and population both feasible and worthwhile.[8]

This understanding of national security confronts the leaders of Third World nations with a very real dilemma—they must provide for defense *and* development in order to be secure. If for industrialized nations the requirement for security simultaneous with economic growth appears difficult, for developing nations it appears impossible. Third World leaders must choose between immediate demands for security in the form of national defense and the long-range requirements for national security through economic development. Failure to accomplish the latter often exacerbates the immediate security problem, and given the fragile state environment described above, most leaders opt for defense over development. As they see it, if they fail to provide for immediate security, they will not be around to enjoy the benefits of eventual economic success, should it eventually occur.

It is easy for those in the industrialized world to criticize such compelling decisions as mortgaging the future for some short-term benefit. But it is precisely the African leaders who must cope firsthand with the increasingly volatile and violent political environments of Africa and the Third World. The point is very simple: Not only is security or defense necessary as a precondition for economic development, as many point out,[9] it is also seen as a vital prerequisite for the continued existence of many Third World countries. Their leaders recognize that defense expenditure might be better spent on development, but only in a perfect world in which defense is unnecessary.[10]

This situation is a paradox, with no simple answer: More defense spending does not necessarily mean more security—in fact it may even reduce it. But by the same token, less defense spending does not automatically mean more development. Nowhere was this situation more evident than in Iran:

> The opportunity cost to Iran of spending more than one quarter of the public budget on military facilities was extremely large and growing rapidly in terms of development and infrastructure projects foregone, social frustration allowed to grow, and political discontent left to spread. The high priority given the military in Iranian public spending (together with the waste, corruption and inefficiency of Iran's public spending in general) seriously drained the resources and the attention that Iranian authorities could have devoted to heading off the wave of political dissatisfaction, including frustration among those groups that traditionally had been the bedrock of support for the monarchy, especially the peasantry, rural migrants, and the lower middle classes in cities.[11]

But such an argument, while intuitively satisfying, lacks an empirical basis. Just as in the preceding chapter it was argued that neither military development nor arms transfers were a guarantee of stability, so one cannot necessarily presume that such expenditures are inherently destabilizing. It might be just as plausibly argued that Islamic revivalism was a response to economic development and modernization, the large numbers of Iranian students educated (and therefore tainted) by the West, or the large number of Western technicians present to operate the modern technology that was imported. Would the ayatollahs have been any less disturbed by the same number of technicians working on tractors rather than tanks? I think not.

There is an element of irony in this issue as well. Within just a few months after the revolution, Iran had become embroiled in a violent, protracted conflict with Iraq. Iran has not beaten its swords into plowshares, but continues to import arms and military equipment. It no longer has the same number of Western technicians, but then again it no longer is the same force that it was under the shah. Its character as well as its capabilities have changed.

The point of all this is simply that arms transfers pose a risk for both supplier and recipient. As indicated in the preceding chapters, African nations are as unlikely to stop demanding arms as the industrialized countries are unlikely to stop supplying them. At issue is the appropriateness of those arms, their impact on the recipient in both the long and short run, and the effect these outcomes have on the interests of the suppliers. The issue is one of much more than politics or economics and touches those elements of society and history that pertain to such subjective elements as national self-reliance, sovereignty, and the ability of national leaders to determine what they perceive as best for the nation's people and their security.

They are not likely to accept arguments that the industrialized nations would or could provide for their protection and thus obviate the need for military expenditures. Not only are military forces a symbol of sovereignty and independence, but more important, they are more reliable in that they will defend national interests as defined by the national leadership. Umbrella defense agreements not only carry with them the potential for uninvited external intervention but also imply that the national interests of both protector and protected are the same. This may have been true during the colonial era, but it is no longer valid today. Often these interests may be similar or related, but will be interpreted and articulated differently, if only to reinforce the independence of the states involved.

Although Third World countries recognize their economic and military dependence upon the industrialized nations, that does not mean that they necessarily enjoy such a relationship or that they do not seek to change its nature. Their leaders recognize, perhaps more realistically than our own, that the perception of threats differs with the interests being threatened, and what appears insignificant to us may be vital to them.

Arms Transfers and Production

It is for this reason, among others, that the developing nations seek the transfer not only of arms but also of the technology needed to support and produce them locally. Although part of an overall program of industrialization, such efforts have an important security dimension that goes beyond the production and substitution of various military consumables and durables to include the research, development, production, and fielding of indigenous weapons systems. As one analyst has observed; "Third World decision-makers perceive an indigenous arms industry as providing at least a partial answer for meeting their national needs. Indigenous defense production is an expression of national sovereignty . . . even if only symbolic."[12]

Arms as Symbols

There are any number of reasons why this desire for indigenous production occurs, but in this context—arms transfers to Africa—there is something especially important in the way that decision makers in both supplier and recipient nations look at the world. It influences their thinking and makes them ignore the long-term effects of their decisions. That "something" is the essentially symbolic nature of arms transfers in international relations. Perhaps Julius Nyerere has said it best:

> The selling of arms is something which a country does only when it wants to support and strengthen the regime or group to whom the sale is made. Whatever restrictions or limits are placed on that sale, the sale of any arms is a declaration of support—an implied alliance of a kind. You can trade with people you dislike; you can sit in conference with those nations whose policies you abhor. But you do not sell arms without saying, in effect: "In the light of the receiving country's policies, friends and enemies, we anticipate that in the last resort, we will be on their side in the case of any conflict. We shall want them to defeat their enemies."[13]

Although supplier nations may not intend such an interpretation of their actions, it is understandable that both recipient nations and others may see them in such a light. Supplier nations are concerned with developing influence in the region that will positively affect their interests, in the form of leverage with recipients. While responding to their demands, however, they may be creating unintended symbolic linkages that are more important than the arms transferred. In other words, it is more important that the United States, the Soviet Union, or France, for example, respond to the demand for arms—demonstrating to both friend and foe alike the special relationship that exists between supplier and recipient—than it is that they actually supply them. As a recent Pakistani pamphlet described the U.S. sale of F16s, "The United States readiness to sell these aircraft represents a symbolic gesture inasmuch as it underlines American commitment to strengthen Pakistan's defenses in a dangerous environment."[14]

There are other subjective elements involved as well, such as the speed and the quality of the response, that are indicators of the nature of that special relationship. But more important is that the relationship exists, thus not only cementing the regime's hold on its position but also reinforcing its image of itself. In fact, this need for symbolic linkages is so strong that a nation will actively seek multiple suppliers of arms precisely because such a strategy will increase the number of its symbolic allies. This course is often taken with full recognition that at the global level it may in fact alienate one or another previous supplier and at the grass-roots level cause serious problems of rationality of equipment, training, and logistics.

The problem of multiple suppliers will be addressed in another context below. Here it is important to recognize that political actors, especially those in the developing world, manipulate their own perceptions and those of others of political and military events and activities. They tend to base their demand for arms on their own perceptions of military threats, rather than on any estimates of their own true military vulnerabilities. Very often, fully aware of the global perspective of the supplier nations, they will couch their terms in global rather than grass-roots contexts in order to generate more willing support.

Thus we find Sudan seeing itself threatened by Libya, despite most analysts' assessments that the Libyans would be unable to seriously damage, much less invade, the Sudan.[15] Yet air raids on Khartoum, which might do little more than superficial damage to either population or property, do threaten the stability and credibility of the Nimeiry regime. The notion of a Libyan juggernaut (supported by the large numbers of weapons possessed by that country, which it has neither the manpower nor infrastructure to support in combat) plays well to both domestic and foreign audiences. For the former, domestic economic difficulties can be laid at Colonel Qaddafi's doorstep, and for the latter, the situation can be offered as an opportunity to counter Soviet or surrogate adventurism in the region that threatens Western interests.

In addition to the threat/vulnerabilities dichotomy, many African and other developing nations are more concerned with creating a symbolic deterrent than with enhancing their military capabilities. Although a large, lightly armed, and highly mobile force may be the most capable in terms of meeting internal threats (by projecting force within its boundaries in all parts of the state) and of defeating an external invasion of territory, the symbolic value and content of such a force is too diffuse, and therefore not much of a deterrent. Again, with reference to the Sudan and its acquisition of U.S. M60A3 tanks, self-propelled artillery, and armored personnel carriers, "the arrival of some new equipment is expected to ease some anxieties in Sudan and, more importantly, give its belligerent neighbors second thoughts about an invasion."[16] In the case of Pakistan, its decision to modernize its air force with U.S.-built F16s reflects this symbolic element as well. As General Zia stated, "Of course 40 planes cannot make all the difference, but the presence of a superior aircraft gives you at least that much more moral as well as military ascendance."[17]

A smaller, mechanized force concentrated in the capital city, although it may be less capable (and in fact may be much more vulnerable to attack), does serve as a powerful deterrent to internal factions (although the army itself may be the breeding place of discord) and to external enemies. The symbolic value of such a force parading on independence day should not be disregarded as a sign of national sovereignty or as a demonstration of the potent response an invader might meet. But by the same token, it should not be overrated and presumed sufficient in the face of the actual military vulnerabilities of a nation or the capabilities of its enemies.

As long as all African leaders persist in such interpretations, such deterrence will probably work and is perhaps as good as any other strategy. However, there is some concern that the emerging regional military powers and extraregional powers may be more likely to intervene militarily in the region; to them, such symbolic gestures are insignificant and are unlikely to deter them.

The New Conventional Weapons

In this environment, the new conventional weapons represent an important element. Despite problems of absorption and employment, they appeal to African nations because of their deterrent value—not because they would necessarily improve military capabilities or reduce vulnerabilities. They serve to threaten and thus deter neighbors or others who might entertain thoughts of interfering in local issues or engaging in attempts to redraw the map of Africa.

Although there are conflicting assessments of military operations of both sides in the Falklands war, already many have concluded that the conflict, brief as it was, is testimony to the effectiveness of new conventional weapons. This will be discussed in more detail in the following chapter, but it would be safe to say that the publicity surrounding that conflict will only add to the demand for such weapons in Africa. Whereas African governments often demanded new conventional weapons in the past, they frequently had to be content with what supplier nations would provide. Since the regional military powers are sure to acquire new conventional weapons in large numbers throughout this decade, in order to deter these symbolic threats, other nations will find that they *must* have them.

There are a number of reasons for the superior symbolic value of new conventional weapons. First, both new conventional weapons and the systems required to deliver them are very expensive, regardless of their source or type of payment required for their procurement.[18] Second, they are state-of-the-art systems and thus the most modern and prestigious weapons available. Third, they are, when properly operated and employed, the most lethal weapons available, and fourth, they are virtually the same weapons as those of the superpowers that manufacture and supply them. Fifth, because they are so expensive, modern, lethal, and similar to those of the modern military powers, their procurement represents in vivid terms the commitment (whether intended or not) of the supplier to support the recipient. Sixth, since they will require the foreign training of local nationals overseas and the provision and presence of what have come to be known as "white-collar mercenaries" to maintain them, these systems provide recipients with the means to manipulate their relations with these persons to achieve other political ends.

The demand for new conventional weapons goes beyond the simple desire for prestige on the part of developing nations. As discussed above, the acquisition of these systems means much more in terms of their security value (no matter how fragile that value might be) and what they represent in terms of the recipient nation's relations with their supplier. They represent, for their recipients, a firm, visible commitment of a more powerful, industrialized nation to the survival in both real and symbolic terms of an African regime. Thus the greater the value or weight of that commitment, the stronger the tie that then can be used by the recipient in further relations with the supplier and other nations. For African nations, so long and so greatly dependent upon other states, it is an opportunity to work the relationship to their advantage: In terms of arms transfers, Africa is not as politically dependent upon the industrialized nations as they are upon it.

Ardent supporters of the transfer of new conventional weapons argue that they represent perhaps the best way of gaining influence in the developing world. Such an approach ignores the fact that recipients appear much more adept at manipulating arms-transfer relationships. Another problem is that by ignoring the long-term, grass-roots problems that the weapons engender, one may overlook that the short-term benefits that they seem to gain may be far outweighed by their long-term costs.

There are two additional dimensions to new conventional weapons. First, since most developing countries seek to modernize their armed forces but can afford to do so perhaps only once through the end of the century, they naturally seek the most advanced weapons possible so that they will "last" or at least not be totally obsolescent in the year 2000. Again, as General Zia has stated; "Pakistan's military inventory is of Korean War vintage. We are not producers of military hardware, and we cannot afford to go out every two or three years and buy new equipment. We have to look ahead for 20 years."[19] The second dimension deals with arms control and is perhaps the most ironic aspect of new conventional weapons. Although arms in and of themselves may not destabilize regional balances of military power, the *perceived,* or symbolic, potency of state-of-the-art weapons is such that nations not possessing them will feel the need to acquire them, even if in reality their own more conventional forces are superior in total combat effectiveness.

The Economics of Arms Transfers

The economic condition of African nations is well known and will not be described in detail here.[20] However, it should be underscored that African nations are some of the poorest in the world and are currently experiencing severe financial difficulties. Dependent primarily upon commodity exports as a source of foreign exchange, these nations find themselves with serious balance-of-payments problems and increasing external foreign debt to both public and private lenders. Given such an environment, it is perhaps the economic impact of transfers of new conventional weapons that is the more serious and has severe political implications for African countries. As one analyst has stated:

Military aid programs provide the greatest, and certainly the most obvious, misapplication of Western technology in the underdeveloped countries. It is a familiar, and now well-documented, fact that American military aid has strengthened the relative position of the armed forces and that increased technical sophistication of new weapons systems encourages armies to draft the already educated urban population rather than take the slow but socially useful route of training the rural youth up to modern standards. But apart from this contribution to the militarization of development, the sheer technology of modern weaponry imposes burdens on low-income countries. Every advance in weapons systems adds to the cost, reduces the flexibility, and increases the sophistication or operational complexity of a nation's military program, without necessarily increasing its security value. The cost of the international "shopping list" of basic weapons available to the underdeveloped countries rises at a greater rate than the levels of inflation as technical improvements are introduced from year to year. For the same reason, the prospects for technical "spillover" from military to civilian uses, one of the supposed side benefits of military aid, are reduced at each advancing stage of sophistication in weapons system technology. Communications and radar technicians are scarcer and probably less likely to moonlight as adult literacy teachers than are cryptographers and motor pool sergeants; and the technicians of modern aircraft maintenance are less available to repair bicycles and plows than were the machinists of a generation ago. The paradox of less security for more money, already familiar enough in the United States and the Soviet Union, is being exported as rapidly and efficiently as the aircraft and tanks that are passed from hand to hand down the ranks of nations eager for military modernization.[21]

David K. Whynes, in his study of *The Economics of Third World Military Expenditure*,[22] has identified seven reasons for the growth in military expenditure in developing nations, and each will be discussed below.

1. The Growing Perceived Need for Enhanced National Security

As indicated in the two preceding chapters, there is considerable evidence to support the contention that pull factors are stronger than push factors in arms transfers to Africa. This is generally true of the developing world:

> Most developing countries, particularly those which have the resources, are preoccupied with the acquisition of weapons, and build up armed forces with the dedication of converts. The people, at least the more articulate classes, in the developing countries have come to believe that their security and future depend entirely on having a large and well-equipped army, whatever the cost.
>
> Indeed, it is unpatriotic to question how much is being spent on defence. Security and armed forces have become synonymous and even in countries where there is a relatively free parliament the military budget receives only a perfunctory and respectful scrutiny. In countries under military rule the defence budget remains a mystery, and whatever is made public is often incomplete and unreliable. Any suggestion that expenditure on the armed forces should be reduced is dismissed as being enemy-inspired.
>
> It is recognised that the process of development could be accelerated if some of the military expenditure were diverted to the social sector but it is considered highly injudicious, if not treasonable, to weaken the defence services.[23]

2. The Increase of Internal Repression

It is often presumed that military expenditures and arms transfers fuel violations of human rights. Certainly such violations do occur and are often perpetrated by military personnel, but it is presumptuous to assume that *all* such violations are the responsibility of *only* the military. Although the line between police and military forces often is not neatly drawn in terms of their roles (especially given the perceived internal threat to security), human-rights violations as they are commonly understood would be most difficult with what is seen as military equipment.[24] In fact, those apparently nonmilitary items of technology such as computers could be more useful in controlling and oppressing dissident populations than tanks or aircraft.

Another aspect of this argument is the notion that military regimes are inherently repressive, whereas civilian regimes are democratic and less destructive of human rights. This is patently false, since the evidence indicates that most militaries want civilian rule, even though "civilian rule does not necessarily mean democratic decision-making."[25]

3. Inefficiencies in the Budgetary Process

These problems, touched on above, are not limited to the military sector in developing countries. They affect developed nations as well. Much of the problem has to do with *accountability*. As one study reported, "Discussion of autonomous agencies would not be complete without mention of the armed forces. If they do not constitute the government itself, they are often a law unto themselves. It is not merely that defense may take a large proportion of a small budget . . . but that these transactions often are not recorded in the regular budget and may constitute the first claims on it."[26]

This is especially true in Africa, where debt and accountability problems both are rampant. As an official of the International Monetary Fund (IMF) told me, it is virtually impossible to assess the financial impact of military expenditures on development because most funding is done outside normal channels, is considered "off the books," and is therefore never made available to IMF. More often than not, when the issue is pressed, figures are fabricated or reflect only domestic military expenditures, not imports, so as to support requests for balance-of-payments support from the fund.

Another problem is that planning in developing countries is a very elastic concept, which does not necessarily drive the budgetary process. A five-year plan often represents a goal toward which the government will work, rather than a realistic objective for that time frame.[27] Often what is budgeted is procurement of new technology or the commissioning of new projects. Recurrent development costs are underfinanced, because investment and recurrent budgeting are separated, future costs are unanticipated or not predicted, there are other demands for funds and only new investment is equated with progress, and projects often ignore underfunding of operating and maintenance costs.[28] These are problems in all sectors, not just the military. And even in the industrialized countries, operations and maintenance are the "softest" and therefore are most commonly cut in military budgets.[29]

Since the military budgets of some African countries are quite high, while others may be underestimated,[30] the absence of effective planning can only make for less security for more money. As one U.S. expert said, criticizing U.S. defense planning, "If you do not plan effectively, the *only* way you can spend money effectively is by accident" (emphasis in original).[31]

4. The Existence of a Military-Industrial Complex

Even though there appear to be growing pressures in some African states for the development of indigenous arms industries, for the most part the region lacks any real "military-industrial complex," excepting South Africa. The military places demands upon domestic production (see below), but the linkage between them appears more accidental than deliberate. More relevant are the costs associated with a standing army. In Africa, "a military establishment has two types of costs, neither of which a modernizing society can afford. An army is not only a heavy burden upon limited financial resources; it also restricts alternative utilization of scarce training facilities and educated manpower."[32]

In fact, since most African nations lack such a complex, "the level of financial expenditure is quite high considering the size of the standing army—in part owing to the need to purchase arms from foreign industrial powers, and in part as a consequence of maintaining an agency capable of maximum coercion with minimum numbers."[33]

5. The Vested Interests of a Military Establishment in These Countries

Recent research indicates that there is little difference in defense spending between civilian and military regimes.[34] Immediate postcoup expenditures are likely to increase somewhat (as happened in Kenya recently),[35] but this may be interpreted in two ways. First, after a successful coup, the military may increase its pay and housing to alleviate the sources of its perceived grievances or disquietude and motivation for involvement in politics. Second, civil authorities may, after an unsuccessful coup or to preclude one, try to buy the loyalty of the army by "keeping the generals happy."[36] In other instances, it may simply be that both civilian and military authorities perceive that the threat demands or the economy can afford such increases. While military expenditures do represent vested interests, they may be those of groups other than the military alone.

Yet such is not always the public interpretation of increases in military expenditure. In Nigeria, for example, the prevalent attitude was: "If the army is not necessary to maintain peace and protect the country, why should it be supported? The general public may not be aware of the extent to which army demands for new equipment are a drain on the country's financial resources . . . , but anyone living near an army base is aware that the men are getting good wages when their official work appears to be nonexistent. The prevailing view is that armies are for war; politicians are for peace."[37]

These sentiments were echoed by a Nigerian official, who summarized the dominant attitude: "In every country the defense establishment is costly to maintain and as this expenditure is not directly productive in the economic sense, there is a tendency, especially in times of peace, to look upon it as a wasteful diversion of resources from more economically and socially desirable goals."[38] And in a recent Zambian parliamentary debate, a member stated that "the government was spending more money on defence than on national development. He said he had an 'uneasy feeling' that Zambia was arming herself against some internal or external enemy and if that was the case, the nation must be told who that enemy was."[39]

6. The Needs of Political Ideology and a Nationalist Identity

The symbolic dimensions of arms (discussed earlier) support this argument. Any attempts to reduce arms transfers—or pull factors—are counteracted by these concerns.[40]

7. Growing Imperialism Among Nations, Including Those of the Third World

This issue has been discussed in some detail in the preceding chapters, but it is significant to note that the threats that seem to be driving the increases in military expenditures are not those of earlier decades—internal subversion and superpower/former colonial power intervention—so much as they are fears of neighboring African states, in particular the emerging regional powers such as Nigeria, Libya, Ethiopia, and South Africa.

While virtually all of these factors apply to African nations, some apply more than others and have already been discussed in some detail. Several additional issues have particular interest with regard to the acquisition of new conventional weapons, particularly as they represent imports (usually on credit) rather than direct military expenditures. Thus to growth in military expenditure can be added the problems of arms imports:[41]

- Arms transfers and imports of supporting equipment distort the trade profile of recipient countries, especially for industrial machinery and transport items (Standard International Trade Classification No. 7)
- Financial flows, including short- and long-term debt, international reserves, cash on hand, and debt-service payments are also distorted
- Military imports are generally of an unproductive nature

- In order to meet the needs of military establishments for more mundane (uniforms, clothing, food) and exotic (repair parts, supplementary equipment) needs, indigenous production is misdirected
- The long-term impact—the way in which weapons systems tend to guide military development—may mean that acquisition of an inappropriate system will result in growth and modernization according to an equally inappropriate model of warfare

In addition, this long-term impact has another dimension because "as soon as a technologically advanced weapon system has been purchased for the armed services, a chain of supplementary import demands is indicated. To remain operational, modern fighter aircraft, tanks or naval units require an extensive network of support facilities, such as a logistical system for the provision of spare parts. For an extended period foreign specialists are required and adequate residential areas must be provided for them."[42]

Furthermore, these imports have important consequences for human resources as well. It is important to note that

> economic considerations include not only resources in terms of raw material and capital, but the skills of the population as well. Security-related programs will usually be competing with the civilian sector of the economy for resources and skilled personnel. The analyst must recognize that, if sophisticated weaponry is furnished, even as a grant, the operation, maintenance and training requirements created will make noticeable demands on the resource market. In the short run, these demands are likely to more than offset the benefits that training on modern equipment may later provide when skills learned in the military service become available in the civilian sector.[43]

Military Expenditures and Arms Transfers

Finally, in addition to the points mentioned above, there are a number of macroeconomic effects on the overall process of social and economic development. But before they can be discussed, it is necessary to distinguish between military expenditures and arms purchases and to point out the relevance of this distinction to the demand for new conventional weapons.

Military expenditures in African countries are almost always domestic expenditures made in local currency and markets. They represent a significant portion of annual government expenditures and it is to be hoped that they are accounted for as part of the overall budgetary process. They are not normally foreign-aid monies, since such loans or grants are earmarked and monitored for particular uses such as balance-of-payments support, purchases of food or equipment in the donor country, or the conduct of a specific project. (See Tables 1 and 2, Statistical Appendix.)

Although the military portion of the budget may not be directly ascertainable, defense spending is most often politically rather than financially constrained. The reason for this is very simple: The monetary policies of most African countries are so loose that additional military or other government expenditures can be financed through an inflation tax rather than with normal revenues. In other words, the government simply prints enough money to meet its defense needs domestically and allows the public to pay for it indirectly through a further inflated and devalued currency. Although this inflation has obvious economic aspects, the issue is the political risks that a government is willing to take by not only tolerating but adding to inflation. Since inflation tends to affect the middle and upper classes disproportionately, such a program of inflation taxing could ultimately lead to the government's alienating its closest supporters and those most likely to support or foment revolution or coups d'etat.

Arms transfers are considerably different. They represent expenditures in foreign markets that must be paid for with hard currencies or international reserves. Although some suppliers, such as the Soviets, have previously accepted payments in local currencies or commodities, they have changed their policies because of the volatile values of such payments and the negative political effects of dumping them on the world market.

Most African countries, even the oil producers, buy arms on credit because of the financial leverage it affords them, and much of the competition among arms suppliers is reflected in their willingness to provide soft, or concessionary, credit terms and rates of interest. Repayments of both interest (debt-service) and principal can cause considerable cash-flow, international cash reserve, and balance-of-payments problems for the purchasers. The challenge for them is to be able to meet short-term financial commitments, maintain and attract further investment and credit, and renegotiate the terms of the arms purchase *after* the supplier nation is politically committed to selling them the arms. Since arms-transfer loans are for purchases in the grantor country only, once such a commitment has been made, the arms producers of the supplier nation act as an influential force to maintain the relationship, even if it appears that the recipient will be unable to pay or is already in arrears for previous purchases. This is a further pressure on African and other Third World countries to buy new conventional weapons— the developed countries produce primarily state-of-the-art weapons systems, and thus it is politically easier to purchase sophisticated weapons rather than more appropriate technology. The supplier governments themselves tend to support such decisions as well, since increased foreign sales of their most modern arms makes their own acquisition unit cost lower and production lines more efficient.

The problems associated with arms transfers are thus deferred to a later date, and for the price of some political concessions, the recipient nation has modernized its military on what appears to be a financially "cost-free" basis. But this is deceptive, since such purchases add to external foreign debt and to debt service, which in both the short term and the long term affect the economic and financial structure of the country. Since debt-service is usually paid with funds generated by exports, radical changes in commodity prices can cause a nation to not meet its total short-term debts for imports.

Nations such as Zaire and Sudan are being required by the International Monetary Fund and other agencies to drastically reform their monetary and economic practices. Resulting increases in food prices bring about urban unrest and may thus threaten the very regime which is to be protected by the arms being transferred.[44]

Although several studies seem to indicate that military development may in fact stimulate domestic demand and economic growth,[45] there is some reason to question whether such demands are for nonproductive uses that further fuel inflation. Also, this stimulation comes from domestic military expenditures, not arms purchases—and since new conventional weapons are capital rather than manpower intensive, local demand is likely to decrease as leaders see these weapons as a way to lower their labor wage bill while increasing military capability.

Although military expenditures are likely to "prime the pump" somewhat and absorb excess local industrial capacity, they may also stimulate growth in unnecessary or inappropriate technologies. The acquisition of more sophisticated weapons will compete with the industrial sector for both capital and skilled manpower. Even though defense expenditures may add to the national industrial base, create additional infrastructure through civic-action and nation-building projects, and provide skills and literacy training for the labor force, it is questionable whether the military is the most efficient means of accomplishing these goals.

Because alternative suppliers of more appropriate arms, such as Brazil, have their own financial difficulties and therefore cannot offer credit arrangements comparable to those of the major arms suppliers, African nations must acquire arms that they can neither afford nor easily absorb. Because of their high political costs, arms are purchased from multiple suppliers, creating what can only be considered a tactical and logistical nightmare wherein rationalization, standardization, and interoperability are nonexistent. Large numbers of advisors and technicians from a host of countries add to the expense of arms purchases and to the confusion.

Conclusions

This issue of appropriateness will be examined in more detail in the following chapter. But at this point, it is important to note that aside from the ability of African armed forces to effectively absorb and utilize new conventional weapons, their societies may not withstand their economic and political side effects. The political economy of new conventional weapons transfers may undermine the very security that arms and military assistance are designed to promote. As Robert McNamara has said, "The point is not that a nation's security is relatively less important than other considerations. Security is fundamental. The point is simply that excessive military spending can reduce security rather than strengthen it."[46]

For nations seeking not only to influence but also to assist African nations in their pursuit of security, attention needs to be paid to these political and economic factors. The dilemma is a very real one—to adequately meet the genuine security needs of African nations (because stability and security will promote economic development) while at the same time not exacerbating political and economic problems through the provision of costly and inappropriate weapons. Thus a more balanced approach must be taken between restraint and pushing arms, recognizing that the costs and *risks* of new conventional weapons far outweigh their benefits and that military aid and development must be more closely tailored to the needs and nature of the recipient country.

Arms Transfers, Technology Absorption, and Human Resources

The art of war, however, as it is certainly the noblest of all arts, so in the progress of improvement it necessarily becomes one of the most complicated among them.

—Adam Smith
The Wealth of Nations, Vol. 2, p. 191

Having outlined in the preceding chapter the costs of transfers of new conventional and other weapons to Africa, it is necessary to assess in more detail their potential benefits. In other words, to make an objective cost- or risk-benefit analysis, one must attempt to measure the advantages and disadvantages that such weapons afford their recipients in military or security concerns.

To do this, I will examine arms transfers to Africa as technology transfers and measure their benefits against the ability of African armies to absorb and effectively utilize them. As indicated in the preceding chapter, it appears that the potential military value of these weapons can be realized only occasionally and at significant additional cost to the using country. Therefore, even though it appears that the symbolic military capabilities of African armed forces may be improved by their acquisition of weapons, such advantages are for the most part temporary or illusory. Very often, the weapons are never adequately absorbed or properly employed, and their contributions to military development are so degraded by social, political, economic, and environmental conditions that they have been as ineffective as other attempts to transfer sophisticated technology to Africa.

Arms Transfers as Technology Transfers

The arms trade with developing nations represents an important source of technology transfer at two levels. First, the weapons themselves require the transfer of operational, technical, logistical, and management skills for their maintenance and employment. Second, through repair, training, administrative, and supply facilities developed within recipient nations, these transfers represent an additional increment of indigenous absorptive capacity and infrastructure.

These developments have particular significance for both supplier and recipient nations and weigh heavily in their measurements of the potential costs and benefits of arms transfers. This chapter examines the types of technology being transferred as part of the arms trade and the impact of these transfers on the human resources and manpower base of recipient countries. It examines in some detail the human factor in military development and stresses the importance of individual and group skills in determining technology absorptive capacity, the importance of indigenous defense industries, and several reasons for the growing demand for such capacities in developing countries.

Arms Transfer Trends

A number of dominant trends have emerged in the international arms trade over the past decade. First, there has been a definite increase in the total dollar value of arms transferred and the number of weapons systems supplied. Second, developing nations, including some of the poorest countries, are rapidly becoming the major consumers of arms. Third, and as a result, virtually all arms suppliers sell weapons on credit with concessionary terms or on a cash basis. Military grant aid, even on the part of the Soviets, is rapidly becoming a thing of the past. Fourth, the weapons transferred are often state-of-the-art systems, as sophisticated as those used to equip front-line NATO and Warsaw Pact units. Finally, several African countries, especially those that have become emerging regional powers, have sought as part of the arms-transfer process to develop their own arms industries and a degree of military self-reliance.

These trends have a great deal of political significance for both supplier and recipient nations and represent much more than the sale of equipment. In fact, they represent a wholesale transfer of modern military technology (in its broadest sense), which may cause a major reorganization of global and regional relationships.

Recipient nations have traditionally sought weapons to enhance their own security and to further their own political ends. This has most often meant the maintenance of internal stability, the deterrence of regional rivals with irredentist or other goals, the symbolic representation of national sovereignty, or the support of aspirations of becoming a regional power. Supplier nations, on the other hand, have used arms transfers to further their own political and economic goals, recognizing that arms transfers are an essential instrument of foreign policy. Local or regional demand factors are rarely taken into account from the perspective of the recipient; rather they are seen as possible constraints on the use of arms transfers to gain regional political influence.

Although there are certainly a multitude of potential buyers, the number of competing potential suppliers has also proliferated. As a result, not only has the arms market become a buyer's market, but in many ways recipient nations have become adept at manipulating arms-transfer relations to their own advantage. This has been manifested by the trends described above wherein the recipient nations have been able to *demand* arms on generally more generous and concessionary terms and in quantities far exceeding those desired by the suppliers themselves.

Military Technology Transfers

Perhaps more important than the direct political consequences of the trends in arms transfers is their significance as technology transfers. Although military technology transfers may be viewed as part of an overall process of the transfer of technology to the developing world, they have a number of facets that distinguish them from nonmilitary technology transfers.

First, most military technology is nonproductive, contributing relatively little, and that indirectly, to the overall national economy of recipient nations. Although some military forces and their equipment are adaptable to civilian, civic-action, or nation-building uses, many are not. The growth of military forces and accompanying increases in domestic military expenditures may stimulate growth through increased demand, but may also add to inflation. The added external foreign debt and annual debt service that arms purchases represent in scarce hard currencies add to balance-of-payments and other financial problems.

Second, military technology is designed to be put to military uses. Even if only intended for its stabilizing, deterrent value, such technology may lead to regional arms races, increased conflict (both in frequency and ferocity), and employment against the force of the nation that originally supplied them.

Third, because of the technology-absorption problems that recipient nations experience, they become dependent either upon large numbers of "white collar mercenaries" to maintain (and even operate) weapons systems or send large numbers of trainees to supplier nations. These expensive, short-term solutions to the problem cause domestic political and economic difficulties and are subject to phenomena such as the "brain drain," the inappropriateness of training, and neocolonialism.

Finally, military technology has peculiar security aspects. The transfer of state-of-the-art equipment to developing nations may speed its compromise (in addition to the loss of proprietary information). Coproduction of, or large stocks of, spares and ammunition permits recipient nations to covertly avoid end-use agreements and retransfer military technology to embargoed nations. This reduces the usefulness of arms transfers and "spare parts diplomacy" as a foreign-policy tool, by reducing recipient nation dependency.

The Nature of Military Technology

The principal problem confronting the consumers of military technology is one of technology absorption. This problem, although remarkably similar to absorption of technology in general, does have some peculiar characteristics worth noting.

First, military technology and the skills associated with its use have a somewhat paradoxical relationship with the civilian sector. At the same time that many military technical skills are readily transferable to the civilian economy, many are not. Unfortunately, it is often the skills that require the most expensive and longest training and experience that are most transferable. In those cases, developing countries are unable to hold on to military personnel so trained. But there are many skills, such as tactics, gunnery, and so on, that are just as essential to proper military technology absorption, but that are not transferable. This confronts many developing countries with a very difficult situation. They must either increase military pay (meaning an increase in domestic military expenditures) to hold on to skilled personnel or lose them. But they very often cannot afford or justify having a large military training establishment simply because the economy can absorb only so many highly skilled individuals and many other "skilled" individuals not at all.

Second, the apparent solution to this problem is to hire technical representatives as part of the credit-based arms-transfer agreement. But this only delays the problem a few years and does not make any lasting contribution to the national economy, labor force, or military infrastructure. It may just as easily cause political problems as a visible sign of foreign dependency and further disrupt import flows as the domestic and support needs of these technicians are met.

Third, there is the question of the overall appropriateness of the weapons themselves. Are they really worth the bother in terms of added military capability, or are they just prestige weapons? Are five F5s properly absorbed, operational, and fully employed in the end more effective than one F15, grounded for parts or flown by only a marginally competent pilot?

Finally, is there such a thing as "appropriate" military technology? There is little reason to believe that such equipment exists currently or that there would be much demand for it. However, with the increase of alternative producers in the world arms market, such equipment may become more available at prices affordable to the poorer nations.

Defining Absorptive Capacity

The ability of a recipient country to absorb military technology is constrained by two critical factors—infrastructure and human resources. The former essentially refers to the larger infrastructural network of a nation, to include the bureaucratic and administrative capability of the government. The latter refers to individual and small-group skills and abilities to actually operate and maintain the transferred equipment. It includes those who have physical contact with the equipment in some capacity and those upon whose actions the actual operators depend. Thus, the ability of an ammunition handler or supply clerk is just as important to absorption capacity as is the gunner who must fire a weapon. Small groups are important because many military systems depend upon crews or teams for their operation.

The linkage between these factors and military development was summarized in one study as follows:

> Important determinants of the military effectiveness attained by a given state lie in the degree of development in the economic, educational, social, political, and cultural spheres. Lags in such components of the development process may adversely affect the ability to operate and support modern weapons, or *micro-competence*, and the ability to organize and manage forces for military ends, or *macro-competence*. . . .
>
> Obstacles to the attainment of military effectiveness may lie in the inadequacy of the population base, deficiencies in civilian human capital programs, a civilian economy which competes for talent, social objectives which override strategic considerations in the use of the military, political tests for military jobs, instability of the regime which leads to distrust of independent power centers, and certain attitudes and mindsets which arise out of the traditional culture. (emphasis in original)[1]

One example should suffice to demonstrate the differences between macrocompetence and microcompetence. The United States recently transferred a number of M60A3 main battle tanks to Sudan. When they were delivered, it was discovered that the fifty-five-ton tanks were too heavy to move on existing rail, road, and bridge transportation between

Port Sudan and Khartoum.[2] In addition, the Sudanese army currently lacks personnel sufficiently skilled to operate and maintain the tanks, especially the sophisticated fire-control mechanisms with which they are equipped.[3] This example also demonstrates the interrelated nature of macrocompetence and microcompetence. In addition to a limited transportation network, Sudan also apparently lacks planners and logisticians who could anticipate such difficulties. This is as much a problem of human resources as the other, which could just as easily be attributed to a lack of military infrastructure—modern civilian and military schools to train soldiers in the operation of such equipment.

These problems are exacerbated by the rate of weapons acquisition and the sophistication of the systems acquired. African nations that ignore the imperatives of macrocompetence and microcompetence are likely to experience not only the political but also the military consequences experienced by Iran:

> The concentration on military modernization at break-neck speed through the acquisition of sophisticated foreign equipment has been all the more questionable as a broad national strategy since there is scant evidence that it made sense in even very narrow military terms. Rather a more moderated and balanced approach to military spending would probably have strengthened Iranian defense capabilities as well as freed public resources and talent for dealing with civilian problems.
>
> A more temperate approach would allow the Iranian armed forces to focus their efforts on 1) improvement in the ability to handle equipment already delivered or on order; 2) building a reliable logistics system; 3) broadening repair and maintenance programs; 4) strengthening command and control; 5) conducting more practical exercises and practice operations; 6) hardening military facilities; and 7) extending the road, railroad, and airport networks in a way that would provide major military as well as civilian benefits. While the "nuts and bolts" approach is not as glamorous as simply adding new layers of the latest equipment it would add substantially to actual military capabilities.[4]

These findings are not significantly different from an earlier (1976) congressional investigation of U.S. military sales to Iran:

> Iran is attempting to create an extremely modern military establishment in a country that lacks the technical, educational and industrial base to provide the necessary trained personnel and management capabilities to operate such an establishment effectively. Iran also lacks the experience in logistics and support operations and does not have the maintenance capabilities, the infrastructure (port facilities, roads, rail nets, etc.), and

the construction capacity to implement its new programs independent of outside support.

—Most informed observers feel that Iran will not be able to absorb and operate within the next five to ten years a large proportion of the sophisticated military systems purchased from the U.S. unless increasing numbers of American personnel go to Iran in a support capacity. This support, alone, may not be sufficient to guarantee success for the Iranian program;

—The schedule for virtually every major program except equipment deliveries to the point of entry into Iran has slipped considerably due to the considerations noted above;

—In the face of immense obstacles, our investigation indicated that the Iranian Armed Forces are making a maximum effort to ensure the success of the modernization program; their efforts, however, are hampered because of rapid expansion in the civilian sector as well. The military, for example, has difficulty in matching civilian salary offers to the growing, but still insufficient numbers of trained personnel. . . .

Factors other than operational effectiveness, such as deterrence and prestige, seem to motivate Iran's hardware purchases.

—Iran apparently believes that possession of the most advanced weapons may serve as a deterrent;

—Many U.S. military personnel believe that weapons such as the F-14 aircraft and the DD993 Spruance class destroyers are not very useful to Iran in the probable contingencies that it might face in the next ten years;

—We were told that because of the priority given to "prestige" systems such as the F-14, already trained personnel assigned to other systems that are more relevant to the near-term threats (F-5E and F-4), have been transferred to the newer systems with a resultant unmeasurable degradation in overall force effectiveness;

—Iran's military programs are having a profound effect upon the socio-economic development of the country. Thousands of young Iranians are learning new skills which have applicability to the economy as a whole. The creation of new bases . . . and the expansion of existing ones . . . are resulting in the development of basic infrastructure and the creation of new communities in sparsely populated areas of the country. Thus the bases may be acting as a catalyst for population redistribution and industrial growth.[5]

Each of these points deserves further elaboration, especially as they apply to the new conventional weapons and to Africa. Taken together, they constitute what have come to be called "back-end" problems,[6] where countries possess the necessary money or credit to acquire weapons on the "front-end" of a procurement program, but lack the infrastructure and manpower to absorb them after the sale. As a result of the need for extensive follow-on training and facility development, recipient nations experience a wide variance between operational and nominal inventories. The former refers to the number of, say, aircraft that are flyable, as opposed to the latter, which would be the number of aircraft possessed by the country's air force. For most developed countries, this variance averages about only 10 percent; for most developing countries, and in Africa especially, it is usually in excess of 50 percent.[7]

Inadequate Technical, Educational, and Industrial Base. Military microcompetence is dependent upon this base. In African countries, with literacy rates averaging under 50 percent,[8] it can be considered to be virtually nonexistent—especially since those receiving schooling are the young, and they very often are being educated in irrelevant subjects. "Persons qualified to teach scientific, technical or vocational subjects are almost non-existent in many countries,"[9] and it is in precisely those subjects that Africa's economic and military needs lie.

Low literacy rates are not unknown in developed-nation armies,[10] but the problem is particularly acute in Africa as it affects the capacity to absorb new weapons systems:

> The effective use of military equipment ultimately depends on the user. If technology is too complex for forces who have only minimal training, the potential effectiveness of a military system will obviously not be realized. This factor—the level of skilled manpower in a nation's armed forces—clearly is an additional element to consider when judging the utility of a specific arms transfer. If the forces on the ground cannot handle a given technology, it makes little sense to provide them with such technology.[11]

> The transfer of a particular weapons system does not automatically confer a new military capability on the recipient. It may be the intention, but not always the result. A host of other factors—strategy and tactics, logistics support, training levels, and so on—must be considered in assessing the effectiveness of a nation's armed forces, and the impact of a particular military procurement.[12]

Such other factors of military development are critical and bridge the gap between macrocompetence and microcompetence. Especially important is the *organizational* capacity to absorb technology. As one study found: "Zaire's poor military performance has led officials to reassess the feasibility of improving Zaire's armed forces. Analysts now question whether they can absorb advanced arms, and suggest that unless the army is completely reorganized, it is unlikely to become an effective fighting force."[13] Zaire is not alone in this situation. Libya, Sudan,

Somalia, and other nations have all experienced difficulty absorbing military technology,[14] and recent Zimbabwean confidence that "we already have tanks in this country . . . and they are being maintained. We have personnel in defence who are qualified to maintain tanks of any description . . . we have no problem in that regard"[15] seems a hollow boast, based primarily on the remnant of the old Rhodesian army that possessed such skills and on intensive North Korean technical assistance.

Underdeveloped Logistics and Maintenance Infrastructure. This problem is endemic in Africa in all sectors and is the basis for developing military macrocompetence. Preventative maintenance at the operator level appears to be an alien concept, and logistics systems upon which good maintenance is based are almost nonexistent. As was found in the Sudan, "A team of U.S. experts due here next year will find that it has to help create a logistics system from scratch—since 'the concept of numbered parts in numbered bins is completely unknown here,' according to a western official."[16] "The normal thing to do in Africa" involves cannibalization of inoperable equipment to keep others running, since the administration of an efficient spare parts systems appears to be impossible in many African states.[17]

Many of the inefficiencies exist for social and political reasons rather than inability:

> Supply systems provide ample illustration of organizations where traditional patterns of authority have constrained efficient performance. The reluctance to release accumulated hoards, the insistence on face-to-face transactions, the fascination with forms and stamps, and the disposition to seek higher level approval for trivial decisions means, for example, that a parts inventory may remain in excess in one location while equipment is grounded for want of the same item at a nearby base.[18]

These problems are only exacerbated by interservice rivalries that produce inefficient duplications of effort in which ground, air, and sea forces insist on separate-but-equal facilities for the same or similar equipment, while other problems go unfunded and thus unresolved. In addition, because of multiple sources of arms, many systems are incompatible, and technicians are unable to develop a needed experience base for similar types of equipment. This is essential for depot maintenance and the ordering of spares and scheduling of repairs.[19]

Such synergies of maintenance and logistics extend into the operational realm as well. Experience in the Iran-Iraq war indicates that "developing nations have almost as serious a problem in learning how to operate as air forces, as they do in learning how to operate and maintain individual aircraft. Sheer numbers of aircraft tell little about military behavior when nations lack overall command and control structure, and tactical and strategic planning capability, to operate their aircraft as part of a coherent concept of operations."[20]

Despite earlier claims that the military is the most cohesive, rational, and technically oriented institution in African societies, there is little evidence to support this notion. In fact, where evidence is available, the performance of the military has been quite the opposite.[21] Although the military may be *more* organized than other African institutions, such a generalization is relative—it does not implicitly mean that it is therefore capable of performing in ways equal to the challenges of military technology absorption.

The Need for Foreign Technical Personnel. A recent study of the Kenyan army concluded that "like other African armies it suffers, but to a lesser extent than most, from a lack of well-educated personnel to fill technical ranks. There is always a shortage of competent, skilled NCOs and only a limited number of suitable candidates come forward as candidates for commissions."[22] The situation is much worse elsewhere in the region— for example, the Ethiopians, Angolans, and Mozambicans are dependent upon Soviet, East German, and Cuban pilots and maintenance personnel;[23] foreigners, primarily French and Belgian, are considered vital to Zaire's forces;[24] and in Libya, "if the Americans left, within six months, not one Chinook helicopter would be flying."[25]

These examples are not unusual; rather they are symptomatic of the lack of military macrocompetence and microcompetence in Africa. The only way for these nations to compensate for these shortfalls is to hire foreign technicians to aid in the operation and maintenance of sophisticated weapons systems. Several points need to be made regarding these personnel. For one thing, they are not always military personnel. Frequently, in fact, they are civilians who may have had military experience but are now working free-lance or for the producers of weapons systems. Second, these "tech reps" are extremely knowledgeable and very often can achieve significant results in keeping equipment operational and in training host-nation personnel. The issue is whether they are intended to develop host-nation military self-reliance by training them to be self-sufficient or whether they are there to foster continued dependency. Obviously, in the case of the Soviets and their allies, the latter has been the case. While the West may strive for the former goal, very often it fails or finds it prohibitively expensive to achieve completely.

Third, these high costs are due to the expense associated with civilian technicians. For example, U.S. mobile training teams (MTTs) are sent on extended temporary duty to train host-nation personnel in the country. Aside from per diem expenses, they receive no additional pay or benefits.

Civilian technicians, however, receive sizable increases in pay, housing, and educational allowances and other benefits, which makes them cost significantly more. Not only are there cheaper alternative methods of securing technical aid, but the cost of one technician often represents the tuition for several host-nation students. And when the foreign technician leaves, that person's skills leave, too.

Fourth, the obvious solution therefore would be to train more African technicians and to use more military personnel in a country. But these options are constrained by two factors. African nations sending military personnel to the United States or elsewhere for training have to pay, usually in hard currency, the travel and living expenses of their personnel. As a result, many countries send very few personnel (even when they are on "scholarship" through grant-aid programs) and frequently have insufficient redundancy to compensate for course failures, illness, and so on. The other factor is that most African nations and arms suppliers are wary of too large a uniformed military presence in the region. Such a situation smacks of neocolonialism and provides a basis for fears of unwanted military involvement in local conflicts.

Finally, "white-collar mercenaries" are politically reliable. As Kenya recently discovered, soldiers with technical skills and education are more likely to rebel at their low wages, relative both to what they might earn in the civilian sector and to what their unskilled counterparts receive.[26]

Schedule Slippage. Despite long lead times for ordering, producing, and delivering weapons to recipient countries, most of these factors are anticipated and planned for by producer countries. Delays occur invariably when the weapons arrive in country. In addition to the factors described above, which account for them, these delays can be attributed to four more immediate problems.

First, recipient countries fail to recognize that a weapons system is a "complex of interrelated subsystems like an airframe, engine, electronic fire control and navigation equipment, and other elements, to include specially designed ground support equipment and facilities."[27] Thus, a nation does not acquire simply a weapon, but a total system that is costly, specialized, and dependent upon other complementary systems to achieve its intended potential.[28]

Second, the proliferation of sources and suppliers makes standardization, rationalization, and interoperability impossible. This is a problem in developed nations as well,[29] but it is chronic in Africa. For example, Sudan was reported to use eighteen different types of artillery, none compatible with the others,[30] and the transition its air force is making from Soviet MIG21s to American F5s "is going to take time."[31]

Third, the scale of the military modernization program often overwhelms existing personnel and infrastructure with sheer numbers, if not increased complexity.[32] Jet pilots, engine mechanics, and air traffic control personnel are made, not born, and require extensive training. Simply doubling the number of the *same* type of aircraft requires years of training and preparation before personnel and aircraft become fully operational.

Fourth, the rate of modernization is critical. In some cases, long U.S. lead times have worked to the advantage of recipient countries, since they give time to "train up" to the new equipment. Otherwise, a manpower crisis can easily emerge:

> The rapid influx into the less-developed countries of large quantities of modern complex military equipment has demanded military skills that are either in short supply or nonexistent in these countries. This lack of skilled military manpower has posed more serious problems than a similar human resource gap in the economic sector because of the rapid rate at which military equipment has been delivered. The manpower base in these countries has been unable to supply in a short time enough men capable of being trained to command, operate and maintain the modernised military establishments.[33]

Civilian Sector Competition. Both the military and civilian sectors in Africa are in desperate need of skilled labor. For the military, increases in the import of sophisticated weapons have fostered dependency upon the supplier for support personnel, both expatriates and local personnel trained overseas. But the demands of these systems for well-educated, capable personnel as technical trainees and the expense of training them have caused a situation where the military must draw on the small population of literate and educated people and take steps to hold on to them once trained.

For the civilian sector, one of the chronic constraints on increased and sustained economic growth is the shortage of skilled, experienced managers.[34] Many of the infrastructural problems alluded to above can be attributed to this shortage, because African governments have been "skimping on pre-project planning, experienced operational managers and skilled technologists."[35] "In the business sector there is an acute shortage of qualified personnel, engineers, technicians; in government, of efficient administrators and planners; in agriculture, of enlightened agriculturalists, extension workers and farm workers; in education and health, of sufficient qualified teachers, nurses and doctors."[36]

The irony of this situation is that most African nations experience almost immeasurable (or at least unmeasured) levels of underemployment and unemployment. As a recent Government of Kenya development plan stated:

At the same time pressure for employment is increasing, the economy's growth is limited by shortages of available labour. In some rural areas, peak season demands for labour exceed the supply. In industry and in the public service, efficiency is impeded by a shortage of capable management personnel. Government ministries find it difficult to spend the appropriations they are granted, due in part to shortages of technical skills for project implementation. These skills range from highly trained graduate engineer to the technician and artisan. . . . The problem is complex. Idle workers and idle capacity sit side by side. Production and implementation suffer from scarcities of technical skills, at the same time there are empty places in relevant training institutions.[37]

Many of these shortcomings can be attributed to the inappropriate educational systems that existed at independence or were created in the immediate postindependence period. As a result, even though education represents the highest single category of government expenditure for most African nations,[38] it has failed to produce a population *appropriately* educated for the tasks of economic development. Most African nations have

failed to recognize that the requirements for technicians exceed by five times those for top professional workers. Overemphasis has been placed on the university degree, to the extent that the few persons who are qualified to enter technical schools prefer to enter the university because of the prestige and pay bestowed upon the holder of a university degree.

Furthermore, primary and secondary school-leavers find themselves unrealistically applying for very high-paid professional and technical jobs. Most of the drop-outs have been conditioned by the experience of the colonial past and believe that a good job can be obtained by success in school examinations.[39]

This situation was summarized most succinctly by an American acquaintance with extensive African experience in the Peace Corps, Agency for International Development, and Foreign Service. He stated that in his experience, "No African is ever qualified for the job he holds—he is either grossly over-qualified or under-qualified."

In addition to the problem of "the diploma disease,"[40] wherein the educational-occupational linkages are well known to African school-leavers and there are definite status distinctions between manual and nonmanual labor,[41] there is the problem of urban migration. School-leavers tend to move toward the bright lights of the city, where they hope to find prestigeful and remunerative employment, despite the need for them in rural areas.[42]

But appropriate education by itself will not solve the skills shortage. Since most educational programs have been directed at youth, time alone may relieve some of the pressure.[43] But more important are private-sector training schemes directed at the upgrading of employee skills. "Few manpower specialists today believe that schools should be responsible for training skilled or semi-skilled workers for employment in agriculture or in industry. There is general agreement that the schools should concentrate on turning out students educated to the point where they can be readily trained by employers for the jobs that need to be filled."[44]

While many manpower experts claim that military training programs are good *potential* suppliers of trained manpower, there is some reason to question this. First, if the military is such an excellent training base generally, why do most nations attempting to reduce the size of their armies offer demobilization programs designed to train soldiers for civilian jobs?[45] Second, although many soldiers receive some transferable training, the most important training is programs that increase literacy— but is the military the most efficient means of accomplishing this educational task? Third, while many veterans do leave military service equipped with marketable skills, they tend to work in the "informal sector," unlicensed and uncontrolled by the central government—"illiterate, unqualified, but equivalent" to those with more formal education and training.[46] Finally, despite all the fanfare associated with military training, "a great deal of effort is directed to modernizing the military . . . [but] . . . too little attention has been paid to the linkages that exist or can be established between the development and utilization of skills in the military and in the civilian sectors."[47]

In other words, military manpower is neither looked upon nor managed as part of the overall development process. Just as military expenditures tend to be "off the books," so too are the skills and training that soldiers receive. Since virtually all African armies are voluntary, they have the pick of applicants and can skim off the best qualified. Once these personnel are trained, they do what their U.S. and other counterparts do and move to the private sector for higher pay and other perquisites— but only on a haphazard and uncoordinated basis and often without the military training of or anticipating the need to train a replacement.

A related planning issue is one of degradation, both external and internal. Armed forces of virtually all nations can expect to lose skilled personnel to expanding industries in need of already trained specialists. A good example of this in Africa has been the civilian airlines,[48] which have drawn pilots and ground crew from the military, as the only source of trained African (rather than expatriate) manpower. These losses are a contribution to development, but a serious loss to the armed forces if they lack a continuous replacement training program.

Although manpower losses to the private sector can be attributed to relatively low military pay and the attractiveness of private employment, they cannot be blamed on military mismanagement, although failure to provide for replacements can be. What is much more serious in light of the increasing sophistication of arms being transferred to African states is the internal degradation problem, wherein the most prestigious, sophisticated equipment bleeds away the most qualified labor to operate and maintain it. Studies in Iran

> revealed shortages of trained pilots and trainable candidates, shortages of instructor pilots, shortages of ground crews and maintenance personnel, and severe difficulties for the logistics system in locating and providing spare parts to individual units. On the one hand, the training of new pilots was not able to keep up with the expanded number of planes. On the other hand, the arrival of new generations of aircraft frequently resulted in a degradation of military capability as the best pilots from existing programs were devoted to new programs.[49]

This is clearly a case of poor defense planning. The end result is an air force that possesses two or more series of aircraft, neither of which it can operate or maintain adequately. By skimming the best personnel from existing programs and placing them in aircraft demanding new skills and levels of competence, both new and old programs become managed mediocrities, and military development is retarded or possibly set back.

Cultural Components of Technology Absorption

These problems all take on uniquely African dimensions. The tendency for Africa and Africans to be extremely hard on equipment, damaging it in most unusual ways, is becoming better known.[50] The African environment itself is particularly harsh, and coupled with the absence of a well-developed infrastructure (such as adequate roads and airfields), it rapidly becomes a graveyard for modern machinery. The human aspects of technology absorption become critical in such a setting, since skilled operation and attentive maintenance often spell the difference between a simple breakdown and the total destruction of a vehicle or aircraft.[51] But more important, human resources determine the military capability of a particular country; put simply, no weapon, regardless of its sophistication, combat potential, or degree of automation, is any better than the person who operates and maintains it.

Several recent studies have confirmed this, in both the developed and the developing worlds,[52] and their implications for African military development should not be ignored. The ill-disciplined army of Zaire and the overextended armed forces of Libya have both experienced difficulties with more sophisticated weapons, but even the smaller, more professional, and better-trained forces such as those of Kenya have had some difficulty.[53]

Problems of technology absorption do not originate only in the size and experience of African armed forces or in the inadequacies of the existing educational systems of the region. Rather they are caused by fundamental cultural and cognitive differences that must be overcome as part of the process of technology absorption. Modern military technology is a product of, and therefore a part of, the industrialized world. Industrialization is in essence a process of acculturation,[54] and the move from village to barracks is as great as that from farm to factory.[55]

Research regarding education, culture, and cognition indicates that human culture and its categories are acquired through learning after birth.[56] Therefore, the world view and ability to comprehend (and subsequently to absorb) technology possessed by an individual is a function not only of his or her innate ability but also of the environment in which he or she is reared. Cognition, especially, is not innate or automatic, but instead is linked to the kind of environment in which it is learned. For example, pygmies from the tropical rain forests of Zaire often make errors in depth perception when out of their normal environment.[57]

This phenomenon is in no way a reflection on intelligence or cognitive ability of an individual, race, or class. Instead it is a simple recognition that deprived of opportunities to learn or experience certain types of behaviors or ways of thinking, children grow into adults who will have subsequent difficulty when confronted with such novel situations. To say that Africa has generally a "scientifically illiterate population"[58] is not to denigrate Africans, but to recognize that a "sense of the machine" must pervade a society as a prerequisite of technology assimilation— that is, it must be learned as part of one's culture.[59]

As Robert July has pointed out, "the African technology" is not backward, but the result of historical choices of technological methods affected by land, subsistence, and marginal utility.[60] In essence, what was rational in precolonial times has been inherited as part of African traditional culture and without reference to its appropriateness in an industrializing society. As a result, there has been a "relatively low daily exposure of the African youth to tools and things mechanical,"[61] and a corresponding difficulty associated with tasks utilizing them. Again, this is a result of exposure rather than intelligence:

An anthropologist, Roy D'Andrade, found that a group of Hausa boys in northern Nigeria did woefully on a part of a test designed to measure abstract conceptual ability. D'Andrade, realizing that white American children actually if not purposefully train intensively for these tests through the toys they play with, gave the boys less than two hours training in the conceptualization of geometric designs, the subject of the test. At the end of that time, he tested them again and found their scores had more than doubled. It was clear that innate capacity had little to do with the group scores.[62]

What delays agricultural and technological progress in Africa is the problem of cultural adjustment to technology from the industrialized world.[63] If the plow has only recently been introduced to Africa, then it should be expected that high performance jet aircraft may be somewhat difficult to properly absorb. As one instructor pilot told me in Kenya, "How can you expect someone to become a fighter pilot in a few months if he has never even driven a car before?"

But problems of this kind may be short-lived. The massive educational programs for both youth and adult literacy may significantly reduce the problems within a generation. Recent research indicates that schooling in literacy is important to abstract thinking, memory, taxonomic clas-sification, and logical processes to include explanation, all of which are critical to industrial skills development and the "sense of the machine."[64] This proves to be an interesting aspect of the trade-offs between defense and development (particularly education). In the middle to long term, African nations may become more secure by slowing their rate of military development (by acquiring more appropriate arms) until such time as more sophisticated and costly weapons cannot only be afforded, but more readily absorbed.

There is a lesson also for those who render military assistance, whether it be training, technical advice, or weapons themselves. "Tasks that seem perfectly simple to one who has mastered them may appear very difficult, and perhaps not worth attempting, to people who have not had the opportunity to master them."[65] Experience in economic aid programs[66] and in recent conflicts[67] indicates that simply transferring equipment is not enough. Cultural and historical factors must be con-sidered before any technological revolutions can be achieved.

New Conventional Weapons and Technology Transfer

New conventional weapons (or precision-guided munitions) seem to offer a solution to the problem of the shortage of skilled manpower. As one analyst observed, "One specific advantage that seems likely to accrue to countries possessing such weapons is the possibility of substituting highly accurate weapons systems for manpower. Many of the weapons are comparatively easy to operate, and thereby require fewer skilled military personnel in the field."[68] But such arguments are deceptive, because "a major disincentive to purchasing significant quantities of advanced weapons for most Third World countries will be the inability to acquire the necessary quantity and quality of skilled manpower and sophisticated support systems to effectively absorb those advanced weapons systems."[69] In addition, "the rapid acquisition of such large quantities of weapons could cause logistics problems even in many developed countries that have a large pool of skilled technicians, good communications and transportation networks, and ready access to ports of entry."[70]

African nations possess a surfeit of unskilled, unemployed, and underemployed manpower. One thing they do not need is military equipment that will conserve manpower—especially if the political and financial costs of the weapons are high, and their acquisition places even greater demands on the small pool of skilled manpower needed for economic development.

Conclusions

Military technology—in particular, new conventional weapons—is not a solution to Africa's growing economic and political problems. But as the preceding chapters have indicated, it is unlikely that the conflicts that will arise will incline African leaders either to sacrifice their sovereignty or to turn all of their swords into plowshares. Rather, what is required is a recognition that state-of-the-art military technology will most likely do more directly and indirectly to weaken African security than to strengthen it.

Military history reveals that technological superiority is a transient phenomenon and that few weapons ever truly revolutionize warfare.[71] Factors such as unit cohesion, training, and morale often are more important.[72] More appropriate military technology, in the hands of soldiers well trained in its use, is a more potent deterrent than prestige weapons. In fact, a more appropriate means may already be in those hands. As one retired African general has said, "Black Africa doesn't stand a chance in a conventional war. . . . Our best chance is to mobilise guerrilla factions to make life impossible for whites in South Africa. . . . This method of warfare is more in line with the relatively low-spending and unsophisticated state of combat groups in Africa. Guerrillas do their job with a minimum amount of equipment."[73] But such an appropriate strategy does not accord with the current path of military development in Africa. Even in oil-producing, booming Nigeria,

> one attractive notion is that Nigeria's trading partners might agree to not sell it really useless things, and thus help to conserve its scarce human resources for developments it actually needs. This has been quietly tried and failed. During the civil war western governments concerted their refusal not to sell the federal government complicated fighting aircraft that Nigerian technicians and pilots could not cope with. . . . In the late 1960s the Russian government sold MIGs to Nigeria, which have since rotted away on the tarmac.[74]

6
Appropriate Military Technology and African Self-Reliance

The nature of the weapon, though it by no means puts the awkward upon a level with the skillful, puts him more nearly so than he ever was before.
—Adam Smith
The Wealth of Nations, Vol. 2, p. 194

Given the types of weapons currently available in the international arms market and African demands for them, it is possible to predict with some assurance the path of military development in Africa. But given the technology-absorption problems discussed in the preceding chapter, it is apparent that more appropriate military technology would aid in directing this process in less disruptive channels.

Experience in past conflicts has shown that with adequate training African armed forces can successfully use weapons in combat.[1] At issue is whether the weapons they are currently acquiring will afford them the same opportunity to "train-up" to newer technologies. In a recent analysis of the African arms market, four distinct trends were discerned in the process of military development:[2]

- The relative position of the military in African society is changing
- The buying habits of the African military are changing and will change dramatically
- Industrialization in Africa will affect the military and will lead to the creation of some local defense industries
- The preoccupation with front-line weapons systems is changing; there is an increasing emphasis on defense infrastructure, training (including formal education within the military), and command, control, and communications

These trends, if they continue, will aid in developing a degree of military self-reliance in Africa. "A self-reliant nation is one possessing a national will to depend as little as possible on external assistance in matters of national defense and internal security."[3] It would be unrealistic, considering the economic conditions in most African countries, to confuse self-reliance with self-sufficiency. The latter is prohibitively expensive, would require a level of industrialization beyond current African means, and would be politically untenable. "Fortress Africa" is virtually impossible given the present degree of international economic interdependence.

Even the newly industrialized nations that have enjoyed successful economic development are not self-sufficient militarily; rather their indigenous defense industries have been built on a firm civilian industrial base and have only now reached the point of coproduction and modification of foreign-designed weapons. In a recent study of those nations, Charles Wolf has found that military development was a critical factor in creating a stable political environment for sustained economic growth. Acknowledging the risks associated with military-supported authoritarian regimes and large military expenditures, he suggests that while such expenditures do detract from economic progress, they become critical only when true political stability is achieved—where armed forces are not necessary to ensure the survival of the government and state. The key to success is to develop *appropriate* military forces, capable of their national security role at minimum cost to the economy. In the newly industrialized countries military development was initially labor intensive, absorbing unskilled personnel, training them, and returning them to the job market. Nations that build up the military with advanced technology, without reference to effectiveness and productivity, will have failed to effectively coordinate military and economic development—*inappropriate* military development is counterproductive.[4]

The situation confronting African states is very similar to that faced by these newly industrialized countries, a dilemma including "the choice between remedying immediate shortcomings or waiting for the appearance of new generations of equipment, or the choice between direct military allocations and a strengthening of the general industrial and scientific base as a condition for future development, or the difficulties about the proper relationship between imports and domestic production."[5]

But the international and regional environments are different now. In the immediate postwar period, military assistance grant-aid programs allowed developing nations to equip their forces at virtually no cost. Today, arms are sold on credit, with resulting economic risks. Furthermore, the nations that largely succeeded on such a path to military development either faced minor external threats or were backed by defensive alliances that included the superpowers. Most African nations have minimized such ties in pursuit of nonalignment and have entered into military aid agreements that do little to deter the growing external threat from neighboring states.

The Appropriate Technology Problem

Clearly, what African states require is more appropriate military technology, suited to states in the earliest stages of industrialization.[6] But finding sources of such technology is a difficult matter. There are three basic approaches to the appropriate technology problem. First, existing technology can be used, and personnel trained to employ it. Second, existing technology can be adapted. Finally, totally new, more appropriate technology can be created.[7]

The advantages of options two and three are obvious. Adapted or appropriate military technology would potentially make greater contributions to the private sector, since the technological level of the military would match that of the society generally. Less-skilled personnel would be employed in the military, absorbing excess manpower that could be trained locally. The technology would have lower unit costs, be cheaper to operate, and require fewer foreign technicians (if any) to maintain. These factors would combine to provide an enhanced military capability, more appropriate to the types and levels of threats an African nation experiences, thus reducing internal and external vulnerabilities.

There would be disadvantages as well. Appropriate military technology would lack prestige value and would not appear to be advancing the level of military or economic development. Since it would entail higher levels of manpower employment, such technology would require larger standing armies, with consequent increases in domestic military expenditures and threats to human rights. Larger armies might also involve greater risks of coups d'etat or disproportionate military influence in government.

Appropriate Technology in Africa

But these points are all largely theoretical, since the absence of appropriate military technology in the arms market, and African demands for it, make such a concept subject to the same limitations as the civilian appropriate technology movement. Intermediate or appropriate technology was first suggested by E. F. Schumacher in his book, *Small is Beautiful*:

> It is vastly superior to the primitive technology of bygone ages but at the same time much simpler, cheaper, and freer than the super technology of the rich. . . .

The intermediate technology would also fit much more smoothly into the relatively unsophisticated environment in which it is to be utilized. The equipment would be fairly simple and therefore understandable, suitable for maintenance and repair on the spot. . . . Men are more easily trained; supervision, control and organization are simpler and there is far less vulnerability to unforeseen difficulties.[8]

But almost immediately, there were operational difficulties with this concept.[9] First, because such technology was labor intensive, it placed a greater demand on an already constrained supply of supervisory and management personnel.[10] Second, newly created appropriate technology was virtually nonexistent and needed to be designed and produced literally from scratch.[11] As a result, appropriate technology was found to be prohibitively expensive, largely because it was itself inappropriate to the existing industrial base. Third, new technology meant new training, and very often students were unwilling to enroll in courses seen as "unmodern" and not leading to prestigious civilian employment. Additionally, schools were already filled to capacity, and no funds existed for another set of technical schools. Finally, no one could be found to teach appropriate technology skills, because instructors were leaving for the private sector or lacked experience in the new technology.[12]

The ultimate irony was simply that those for whom the technology was intended failed to adopt it. As one Kenyan official told me, the only successful appropriate technology project was a UN-sponsored and -run farm outside Nairobi. No one else, especially a poor farmer, could afford, understood how, or even want to do things that way.[13]

Appropriate Military Technology

The suppliers of arms to Africa potentially would experience similar problems with appropiate military technology. Three issues emerge to effectively preclude their reorientation from state-of-the-art to more appropriate weapons systems. First, does a market for intermediate technology actually exist? Given the pressures described in the preceding chapters, it is highly unlikely. Second, assuming that such a market would exist, who would pay the excessive research, development, and experimentation costs associated with it? Ideally, these would be paid for by customers, but at least initially they would have to be borne by supplier nations. Third, how would the industrialized nations effectively support such systems when they themselves do not employ them? In the absence of indigenous spare parts production capacity, supplier nations would need to develop additional logistics support for these weapons.

Beyond equipment, there is the issue of training and its appropriateness. Although certain types of training are readily transferable or are more or less universally applicable, the industrialized countries train their military personnel to operate, maintain, and employ sophisticated equipment in combat scenarios radically different in kind and scope from those found in Africa. Foreign military students experience much the same lack of relevant training as their civilian counterparts,[14] and far from whetting their appetites for sophisticated arms (as suggested in a congressional report[15]), the experience frequently alienates them.

Other factors conspire against appropriate technology and training. Since it would cost supplier nations so much to actually provide, most statements about promoting military self-reliance are more rhetoric than reality.[16] The life-cycle for producing new equipment and doctrine is so long—much longer than for civilian products—that proliferation of low, medium, and high technology systems is simply impractical.[17] Given the human resource constraints mentioned in the preceding chapter, although more appropriate technology in larger numbers might be the rational substitute for more sophisticated systems,[18] it might be more practical to adopt them because of limited piloting or servicing capabilities.[19] Finally, because of the tendency to add capabilities to "simple" systems through avionics and electronics retrofitting, many of the more appropriate systems are just as complex as their state-of-the-art counterparts.[20]

The F5 and C130 Experiences

An excellent example of these phenomena regarding appropriate military technology is the Northrop F5, a jet combat aircraft designed by an American aerospace firm for the export market. The aircraft has gradually evolved through a series of models, with some twenty-eight nations flying the aircraft (with some coproducing it under license) for a total of over thirty-five hundred planes. Significant features of the aircraft are its relative simplicity (fewer parts, lower operations and maintenance costs), lower cost ($7 million each, compared to $12 million each for the F16), and combat potential (high combat thrust-to-weight ratio, modern avionics such as a heads-up display).[21]

But despite its success, use of the aircraft has experienced and continues to experience political as well as other problems. In its early stages, the F5 was transferred to a number of countries under the Military Assistance Program. It was not adopted for use by the U.S. Air Force (although a related aircraft, the T38, became the workhorse of the Air Training Command), but sufficient aircraft were transferred to permit Northrop to recoup its research and development costs and to realize a respectable profit. Additional sales to Middle Eastern nations such as Saudi Arabia and Iran insured its success, especially after the early A and B models (the latter is simply a two-seat version of the former) were upgraded or superseded by the more sophisticated E and F versions.

At the same time, however, during the mid-1970s, several things occurred to cause difficulties for the F5. First, with the winddown of and disillusionment with the Vietnam war, the Military Assistance Program (MAP) began to wane. Now F5s were being transferred mainly as part of the Foreign Military Sales (FMS) program. Second, the U.S. Air Force and Navy were developing new generation fighters, much more sophisticated than the F5. Third, these newer aircraft were available for sale to countries such as Iran, and suddenly the "export-only" F5 lost much of its appeal. Finally, congressional reaction and presidential policy turned against the continued export of arms to developing countries in economic difficulty.[22]

Encouraged by its previous success and the search for an FX (or fighter export) to meet the needs of developing countries for more appropriate technology, Northrop used its profits from earlier sales to underwrite development and production of another model of the aircraft, the F5G (now called the F20). But the company was caught between conflicting political interests: In order to compete with other FX candidates, most notably the F16-79, Northrop had to make the F20 as sophisticated as it could, while still maintaining its reputation for simplicity of operation and maintenance. But by so doing, it ran afoul of congressional apprehensions that the United States would be "pushing" arms too sophisticated for many recipients and violating the Carter administration's policy of arms-transfer restraint.[23]

Since the F16 and other state-of-the-art aircraft are available and even the U.S. Air Force will not buy the F5 or F20,[24] few recipient countries have placed orders allowing Northrop to start up its production lines for the aircraft. In addition, by buying another aircraft, recipient countries are also buying into the support system of the U.S. Air Force for its own aircraft, thus ensuring more reliable and accessible sources of spares and maintenance. Ultimately, these practical concerns are overridden by the political symbolism involved. The F5 series aircraft is unacceptable to countries seeking the "best" that their money or political concessions can buy. And what is a better measure of U.S. support than the transfer of the most modern aircraft?

As a result of congressional indifference, changing arms-transfer policy, and the lack of any aerospace industry constituency for aircraft like the F20 (after all, the really big sales will be made with the most sophisticated aircraft—to both domestic and foreign customers), Northrop and the true FX concept are at risk. The only remaining option is for appropriate military technology to be created by adapting existing technology—it is not economically feasible to create it, like the F5, completely from scratch. Attempts at modification for export, such as the F16-79 (which is the F16, with the less powerful J79 engine), have been largely unsuccessful, simply because it lacks the prestige and power of the regular F16.[25] Despite doubts about the ability of the recipient nations to absorb such technology, the aircraft are transferred just the same, for political and strategic reasons.

The irony of the F5 saga is simply that its being in production offered the U.S. Air Force a source of aircraft in a crisis situation, which would permit a rapid surge in the number of combat aircraft available, with a relatively shorter time required to train pilots in their use.[26] The aircraft has also featured prominently in the military reform movement as part of the quantity/quality controversy, largely because of its demonstrated performance in the AIMVAL/ACEVAL tests conducted against more sophisticated aircraft.[27]

Another example of a more appropriate military aircraft, which has enjoyed more recent success, is the C130 Hercules, a tactical transport aircraft. Of the sixteen hundred built, over half have been exported to fifty-three countries since 1955. Over 75 percent of these were direct commercial sales, with the remainder being transferred through Foreign Military Sales. Unlike the F5, there is virtually no other U.S.-built aircraft to compete with it, and its well-earned combat and commercial reputations continue to boost sales. Of course, as a transport aircraft it has civilian applications and does not suffer from many of the political and arms control considerations affecting a fighter aircraft.

The C130 Hercules has also undergone continuous modification and modernization. In fact, the C130H is more modern that the C130D model that predominates in the U.S. Air Force. As a result of differences in spares and repairs, the air force logistics system is not the preferred method for support. Rather, countries such as Zaire prefer to acquire the aircraft through Foreign Military Sales (on credit) and support directly from Lockheed. Unfortunately, due to lack of credit and foreign exchange, many of Zaire's C130s are nonoperational. In addition, the people and environment are tough on the aircraft, even though pilots sent to Lockheed schools are already multiengine rated.[28]

New Conventional Weapons

Clearly, the preceding arguments indicate the inappropriateness of new conventional weapons for Africa. Despite claims that technology simplifies operation and maintenance and that such weapons are inexpensive—one account says *"only* hundreds of thousands of dollars apiece"[29](emphasis added)—it is obvious that the human and infrastructure resources do not currently exist in the region without significant political and economic risks.

In the United States, the so-called military reform movement in Congress and the defense establishment is beginning to question "our strategy of pursuing ever increasing technical complexity and sophistication [that] has made high technology solutions and combat readiness mutually exclusive."[30] Should these reformers have an effect on defense procurement, it is likely to mean that less complex equipment—and more of it—will become available through the security assistance program.

These arguments have gained further momentum as the results of recent conflicts involving new conventional weapons are analyzed. As one observer has pointed out, "The fighting in Lebanon, in the South Atlantic and between Iran and Iraq has tended to focus public attention on advanced missiles and weapons, on glamorous military hardware. But the combat also seems to underline the importance of such basic military factors as training, tactics, motivation and the skillful use of standard weapons."[31]

Alternative Suppliers

One other possible source of appropriate military technology for Africa is the Third World itself. The newly industrialized countries—Brazil, Argentina, India, South Korea, Taiwan, Singapore, Israel, and South Africa—all have undertaken for a variety of reasons the development of indigenous defense industries.[32] They are currently emerging as significant suppliers of arms to developing (and some developed) nations, primarily because they are available and willing to sell military technology with few if any foreign policy strings. They are able to exploit the competition among the major suppliers and provide arms to recipient nations, the political goals, financial situation, or human rights record of which may deny them access to the principal suppliers.

These arms, however, are not available on credit. Brazil, for example, has its own debt problems and cannot afford to extend credit to its arms purchasers. But the product is certainly more appropriate to African circumstances, keeping both cost and user in mind.[33] "The appeal of the Brazilian product lies in its sturdiness and the relative simplicity of maintaining it—both critical factors in African conditions."[34]

There is little indication, however, that African nations seek the products of these industries as a matter of preference. Developed-nation technology (in particular U.S.) is viewed as superior, but as very expensive. The vagaries of the political decision-making process in the United States, long lead times, and the stringent end-use requirements and openness of U.S. arms purchases are also daunting.[35]

There is currently an opportunity for these producers to succeed in the international arms market, but it may not persist or exist for long or for many more new suppliers. Just as there is a theoretical limit to the number and type of arms that can be absorbed by an individual nation, there also exists a possibility of market saturation on a global or regional level.

Yet many nations continue, for a variety of reasons, to pursue the development of an indigenous arms production capacity.[36] They do so not primarily to add another dimension to their industrial output, but for cogent national security reasons. The development of arms industries often *detracts* from general industrialization by diverting investment, skilled personnel, and other resources. Once committed, these resources may become excess capacity and not transferable to the civilian sector. The opportunity costs of retooling, retraining, and so on would be as excessive as they were originally when the defense industries were created. These industries, and their nations, will have to seek markets to survive.

Whereas many of the present arms producers achieved a degree of industrialization prior to building defense industries, or at least built them simultaneously and in coordination with one another, many nations seek defense industries in the absence of such a base. The oil-producing countries in particular are capable of buying complete factories for assembly and coproduction of defense equipment. Although certain production facilities, such as those for ammunition, would be practical, wholesale purchases of defense industrial capacity without a firm industrial base are simply a waste of money. It would be better spent buying large quantities of spares, building facilities to store them, and training personnel to use them.

Several African solutions also would ameliorate these problems. By concentrating on rationalization, standardization, specialization, and interoperability *within* Africa, it should be possible to cooperate, much as African airlines have in training and in maintenance.[37] Cooperative facilities for rebuilding and upgrading obsolete equipment may be the best goal for incipient African defense industries—to adapt existing technologies to make them suitable for an African environment.[38]

Conclusions

This discussion has by no means exhausted the problems associated with appropriate military technology transfer, but it has pointed out many of the major issues associated with this phenomenon. The question remains, of course, of what the United States and the other industrialized nations do about it.

Clearly, if present trends continue, the international trade in arms will get out of control. The increasing competition among present suppliers, proliferation of new suppliers, and continuing demand for arms in a conflict-ridden Africa will exacerbate this. The United States for its part finds itself unable to unilaterally disengage from the market because of its own policy interests and domestic defense industries.

Certainly a more informed and pragmatic approach needs to be developed toward arms transfers. Transfer of state-of-the-art equipment to African nations is probably ill-advised because of technology absorption problems. Encouraging and in fact financing purchases from new allied suppliers may be a solution. Transfer of production technology should also be limited, if only to slow the growth of production capacity worldwide. Repair, modification, and training facilities should be encouraged, as should the production of supplies and spares, to channel the urge for indigenous defense industrialization in ways that are productive and cost-effective.

Finally, U.S. arms-transfer policy needs to be better informed regarding recipient perspectives on their security needs. If, in addition to furthering U.S. interests, the United States is concerned with enhancing security and stability in the developing world, such perspectives are essential to making arms transfers work as an effective tool of foreign policy. Decisions regarding them cannot be taken quickly or in a vacuum— they are part of the overall economic, political, strategic, and technological relationship between the United States and Africa.

7
Conclusions and Policy Implications

"Defense, however, is of much more importance than opulence. . . . "
—Adam Smith
The Wealth of Nations, Vol. 2, p. 429

The preceding chapters have described a number of features of the process of military development, its nature, and manifestation in Africa. These features also have significant implications for U.S. policy on arms transfers and security assistance to Africa and may be summarized as follows:

- African nations are pursuing through arms transfers a program of military development designed to meet their perceived security needs
- This pursuit is driven by very real military threats in the region and is unlikely to abate until such time as those threats are reduced or an adequate level of military development is achieved
- Despite their very real economic problems, African nations have chosen to seek military and economic development simultaneously
- A large number of nations, including the United States, are willing to assist in this process in order to gain political influence in the region
- Success or failure in this aid will be measured not only in terms of the influence gained, but the degree of military development achieved at a minimum cost to economic progress
- Provision of new conventional weapons to African nations will cause political, economic, and technology-absorption problems that will far exceed their military value
- Thus, while a policy of arms-transfer restraint is infeasible, an unrestricted policy of pushing or providing new conventional weapons to African nations may be counterproductive

- What is required is a balanced policy that meets the genuine security needs of African nations without destabilizing or retarding economic progress

Some Modest Policy Proposals

Recognizing that African nations require, and will inevitably acquire, the means to achieve military development and that those means should be appropriate to their societies in their political, economic, and cultural dimensions, what reasonable alternatives exist for the United States to meet that need? The following proposals suggest some ways in which U.S. security assistance can more adequately meet the defense needs of Africa while maximizing both the short-run (influence and access) and long-run (stability and development) goals of its foreign policy. Many of them will be immediately dismissed as impracticable or politically infeasible—but they are inferences drawn from the preceding analysis and should be seriously considered even in the face of such objections. My proposals are to:

1. Overcome the institutional bias against security assistance for Africa
2. Increase U.S. security assistance in Africa
3. Establish development and applicability criteria for security assistance to each African nation
4. Reform security assistance financing realistically
5. Encourage the development of U.S. intermediate military technology
6. Emphasize aid programs to develop military absorptive capacity
7. Revamp the marketing approach used in Foreign Military Sales.

Overcome the Institutional Bias

Many academics, current and former government officials, and African interest groups persist in the belief that military aid to African nations is not only misguided but morally wrong. They argue that African problems are economic rather than military, that such aid supports authoritarian regimes, and that rather than introducing superpower competition to the region through arms transfers, the United States, the Soviet Union, and their respective allies should and could guarantee the entire continent against subversion and aggression.[1]

Although there is merit to these arguments and certainly some African support for them, they are naive and paternalistic and ignore the forces of nationalism and sovereignty discussed in the earlier chapters as pull factors. Although the Soviets could reasonably be accused of pushing arms in lieu of economic aid, the primary basis for the growth in African arms transfers is simply the African *demand* for them.

Increase U.S. Security Assistance

U.S. security assistance has been "fairly constant and relatively insignificant"[2] over the past three decades. The region currently accounts for about 6 percent of the annual U.S. security assistance budget. This proportion should be drastically increased, even if the budget itself does not expand. The reason for this is very simple—if in fact arms transfers and military assistance are intended as an instrument of foreign policy, nowhere else do they produce such a high return on such a small investment as in Africa. Not only is the African need greatest, but the relatively few millions of dollars (in some cases, few thousands) spent for African security assistance enjoy a sort of multiplier effect in which political stability and U.S. influence are dramatically affected by small increases or decreases in individual country allocations, compared to the billions spent annually for Egypt and Israel.[3] To produce a comparable outcome in the latter countries, massive amounts of money would need to be spent, yet these allocations are considered sacrosanct when choices are made for budget reductions.

However, security assistance increases should not be made at the expense of economic aid; in fact, programs such as the Economic Support Fund should be increased for infrastructural development (to include educational facilities) rather than for balance-of-payments supports and equipment purchases. Security assistance, like foreign aid generally, does not enjoy a great deal of popular or congressional support,[4] and although it is unlikely to be reduced, aid monies need to be reallocated regionally to align them more closely to our own interests and specific needs and to spend them where they are the most productive.[5] By applying more stringent development and performance criteria, it should be possible to insure that aid monies are better spent and to convince Congress and the equally skeptical public that such expenditures are worthwhile. Again, the current 4:1 economic-to-military aid ratio should probably be maintained, but the total amounts increased.

Establish Development and Applicability Criteria

Each security assistance effort should be more closely examined to determine its short- and long-term effects on the recipient country, especially in terms of what one official calls the "criterios of applicability." He suggests that the chairman of the Joint Chiefs of Staff be required "to certify in writing that equipment (for sale to another country) fits with our concept of their military needs and that they could reasonably absorb it in their military structure."[6] Certifications similar to these are already required as arms transfer "impact statements" by Section 202 (b) of Public Law 94-329,[7] but apparently as implemented are not sufficient. Both the Carter and Reagan arms-transfer policies mentioned the importance of such considerations, and each embassy is required to include information in this area in its AISSA (Annual Integrated Summary of Security Assistance) used to formulate the forthcoming security assistance program each fiscal year.[8] But apparently such input is more or less ignored. As one person in the security assistance administrative system stated, "The whole FMS (Foreign Military Sales) system is not interested in feedback information. MAP (Military Assistance Program), yes! But with FMS cases we really don't care if the equipment rots."[9]

Other sources of vital "applicability" data are the security assistance survey teams sent to African and other developing nations. In the case of Zaire, the report of such a team "led to the scrapping of plans which emphasized expensive and sophisticated equipment in favor of a concentration on fundamental needs for defense."[10] But this team and its report were criticized by the Government Accounting Office because the team's recommendations were adopted by Zaire and formed the basis for its security assistance requests![11] Clearly, a more pragmatic and nondoctrinaire approach needs to be taken to security assistance. Such realism would be based on an accurate assessment of what the recipient nation needs for self-defense *and* the contribution that aiding it would make to U.S. interests.[12]

Reform Security Assistance Financing

Given the severe financial difficulties of most African nations, the present policy of emphasizing Foreign Military Sales over the Military Assistance Program should be reversed. Although the Military Assistance Program has been condemned to a slow death by Congress, it should be resuscitated for Africa. MAP essentially lost support because of its perceived failure in Vietnam, the lack of surplus stocks of equipment for transfer, the loss of public support for military grant aid, and the skyrocketing costs of newer weapons sysems (including the new conventional weapons).

Even though it would appear that military grant aid would be more expensive than military sales, in the long run this is most likely untrue, for several reasons. Virtually all sales to Africa are on a credit basis with concessionary terms, renegotiated payment schedules, and ultimately credits that are partially or totally "forgiven." It simply is unrealistic to think that any African nation will be able to repay all of its military sales debts, and given the negative impact of such debts on their finances, it might be better to start off by granting the equipment to them initially.[13]

Such a program would not mean that African nations would have endless arms shopping lists or would not have to pay anything for their defense equipment. One study has suggested that such a military assistance program would underwrite the costs of weapons procurement for the recipient country, which would then be required to pay all operations and maintenance costs. This would put the burden on the recipient country for deciding how to use the weapons and how large their force should be, since support of their forces would then be through military expenditures that would be more or less economically feasible.[14] Since the United States is currently undergoing a massive force modernization program, the depleted stocks of surplus equipment should be somewhat restored to permit MAP grant-aid transfers on a low-cost or no-cost basis.

Specific options to address the appropriate technology issue may include permitting FMS or MAP recipients to use all or a portion of their credits to purchase allied equipment more suited to their needs. Since the United States appears to lack the industrial base and willingness to produce intermediate military technology, it may be more beneficial to allow such purchases. In the event that a U.S. firm would produce these more appropriate weapons, they could be given certain advantages in MAP equipment acquisitions, or African nations might be given incentives to purchase these less sophisticated weapons under FMS on a no-interest or low-interest basis. Allowing FMS customers to buy abroad with U.S. credits would have two additional benefits: It would be an indirect form of aid to allied nations such as Brazil, and it would cause U.S. arms industries to seek to develop more appropriate military technologies in order to compete internationally.

Encourage the Development of U.S. Intermediate Military Technology

This could be accomplished in several ways. First, weapons manufacturers should be encouraged to develop export-only versions of current equipment. Second, an aggressive rebuild and upgrade program could be developed for older or obsolete equipment, using private or government-owned facilities. Again, allies could participate in such efforts, allowing those that are newly industrialized or industrializing countries to absorb their excess capacity.

Emphasize Aid Programs

This problem has two dimensions—infrastructure and human capital—that also have the most potential for development contributions in the economic sector. Rather than concentrating on arms transfers, security assistance should focus on the construction, improvement, and maintenance of multiuse facilities such as highways, communications nets, harbors, airfields, and so on. In addition, more U.S. funds and facilities should be devoted to basic and technical education within African nations generally (using basically the same rationale as U.S. Title VI, National Defense Education Act programs).

Training through the International Military Education and Training program (IMET), mobile training teams, and the provision of U.S. military advisors and technicians should be increased where possible, recognizing both the economic and political constraints in host countries. Emphasis on training will promote military macrocompetence and microcompetence and enhance technology absorption and unit cohesion, recognizing that "many Third World armies need cohesion more than they need weapons and technical skill."[15] Further consideration of the long-term economic effect of military training should also be emphasized, since "tailoring military programs to suit the socioeconomic needs of individual countries can become an important part of development strategies."[16]

Revamp the FMS Marketing Approach

In addition to cooperative agreements with allies,[17] the international market for arms needs to be closely scrutinized and reevaluated. The market needs to be segmented, by region (geographically, linguistically, or historically defined), by per capita gross national product (GNP), by weapons system type (air, land, sea, defensive, offensive, tracked, wheeled, and so on), or by sophistication (high, middle, or low). Only after this is accomplished can a "market-sharing" approach[18] be developed among the Western allies and the basis for a more efficient yet restrained supply of arms to Africa be developed. In addition, by marketing less-sophisticated systems creatively (for example, offering infantry fighting vehicles as light tanks), it may be possible to encourage a degree of realistic restraint on the part of African nations themselves.

Conclusions

The preceding list of options is by no means exhaustive; however, these options taken together form the basis for a new, regionally oriented U.S. arms-transfer policy. This policy would encourage and practice what in essence is a qualitative restraint (limiting the transfer of new conventional weapons), because it is in the interests of both the United States and African nations to limit the political and economic risks of arms transfers.

Yet such a policy would be realistic. It would meet the demand for African military development competitively and insure the creation of some degree of African military self-reliance, while at the same time enhancing U.S. influence and access to this region of increasing strategic and economic importance.

Statistical Appendix

All material in this appendix is drawn from U.S. Arms Control and Disarmament Agency, *World Military Expenditures and Arms Transfers 1971–1980* (Washington, D.C.: U.S. Government Printing Office, 1983).

Table 1. Shares of World Military Expenditures, 1971 and 1980; Average Annual Rates of Change, 1971–1980, by Groupings of Countries

	1971	1980	Average Annual Rate of Change 1971-1980*
World	100.0%	100.0%	2.60%
Developed Countries	82.1	77.6	1.83
Developing Countries	17.9	22.4	5.66
Region:			
Africa	1.2	1.5	6.66
East Asia	10.7	10.8	2.37
Europe	54.3	55.1	2.77
Latin America	1.3	1.6	4.74
Middle East	2.6	6.9	15.50
North America	28.2	22.6	−0.21
Oceania	0.7	0.6	0.44
South Asia	1.0	0.9	2.64
Organization:			
NATO	44.1	38.6	0.88
Warsaw Pact	35.6	36.8	3.04
OPEC	2.4	6.2	15.30
OECD	48.3	42.6	0.83

*The average annual rate of change was obtained by applying a least squares fit to the log form of the following equation for each year of the decade:

$$Y = A(1 + \frac{r}{100})^T$$

where Y is military expenditures, T is time in years, A is the estimated starting point of the series, and r is the average annual rate of change. (In some cases the log form yielded a poor fit to the data. In order to have a consistent measure of change this exponential growth rate formula was used in all cases, however.)

Table 2. Relative Burden of Military Expenditures*

ME/GNP % (1980)	GNP PER CAPITA (1980)				
	Less than $200	$200 – 499	$500 – 999	$1000 – 2999	$3000 and over
10% and over	Kampuchea (75)	Lebanon (77) Mauritania Yemen (Aden)	Yemen (Sanaa) Albania (76)	Syria Iran Jordan	Israel Oman Czechoslovakia Soviet Union Saudi Arabia Bulgaria
5 – 9.99%	Ethiopia Guinea-Bissau Chad (79)	China Somalia Egypt Tanzania Pakistan	Zimbabwe Korea, North Cuba (75) Morocco Peru East Germany	Iraq (79) Taiwan (78) Korea, South	Qatar Austria United Arab Emirates United States Poland Greece United Kingdom
2 – 4.99%	Burma Upper Volta Burundi Mali Rwanda	Madagascar Kenya (75) Angola Mozambique (78) Cape Verde Zaire Sudan India Indonesia Senegal Togo Benin Afghanistan (78)	Equatorial Guinea (75) Congo Guyana Zambia Botswana Thailand Nicaragua Swaziland El Salvador Philippines Bolivia (79)	Malaysia Yugoslavia Turkey Portugal South Africa Nigeria Chile Algeria	Kuwait Romania Hungary France Belgium Germany, West Netherlands Sweden Norway Bahrain Denmark Argentina Italy Australia Switzerland

1 – 1.99%	Bangladesh	Guinea (75)
		Central African
		  Republic
		Malawi
		Liberia
		Haiti
		Sierra Leone
			Honduras
			Uganda
			Cameroon
			Dominican
			  Republic
			Papua New
			  Guinea
			Sao Tome &
			  Principe
				Ecuador
				Uruguay
				Tunisia
				Paraguay
				Ivory Coast
				Venezuela
				Colombia
					New Zealand
					Canada
					Ireland
					Spain
					Libya
					Finland
					Cyprus
					Luxembourg

Less than 1%	Nepal	Sri Lanka Lesotho Gambia, The	Jamaica Ghana Mauritius	Brazil Fiji Guatemala Panama Malta Mexico Barbados	Japan Gabon Trinidad & Tobago Iceland

*Countries listed in columns in descending order by level of ME/GNP. ME/GNP ratios reflect 1980 data with the exceptions noted by years. Data not available for following unlisted countries: Costa Rica, Laos, Mongolia, Suriname, and Vietnam.

Table 3. Shares of World Arms Imports, 1971 and 1980; Average Annual Rates of Change, 1971–1980, by Groupings of Countries

	1971	1980	Average Annual Rate of Change 1971-1980*
World	100.0%	100.0%	7.39%
Developed Countries	26.4	22.0	3.18
Developing Countries	73.6	78.0	8.74
Region:			
Africa	4.6	18.8	33.37
East Asia	33.0	12.4	−9.15
Europe	31.7	21.3	2.44
Latin America	3.7	6.8	15.81
Middle East	18.3	33.1	14.77
North America	2.8	2.4	5.37
Oceania	0.1	1.1	7.62
South Asia	5.0	4.0	6.48
Organization:			
NATO	22.0	12.9	1.70
Warsaw Pact	9.8	7.5	2.46
OPEC	9.0	26.6	24.90
OECD	26.1	17.9	3.65

*The average annual rate of change was obtained by applying a least squares fit to the log form of the following equation for each year of the decade:

$$X = A (1 + \frac{r}{100})^T$$

where X is arms imports aggregates, T is time in years, A is the estimated starting point of the series, and r is the average annual rate of change.

Table 4. Value of Arms Transfers, Cumulative 1976–1980, by Major Supplier and Recipient Country (Million Current Dollars)

SUPPLIER / RECIPIENT	TOTAL	SOVIET UNION	UNITED STATES	FRANCE	UNITED KINGDOM	WEST GERMANY	CZECHO-SLOVAKIA	ITALY	POLAND	SWITZER-LAND	YUGO-SLAVIA	OTHERS
WORLD TOTAL	110,500	38,600	31,700	8,500	5,700	5,100	3,700	2,800	2,000	1,600	1,100	9,700
DEVELOPED*	24,100	5,700	8,900	440	1,000	1,000	2,700	110	1,500	800	30	1,700
DEVELOPING	86,400	32,900	22,800	8,000	4,600	4,100	975	2,700	500	800	1,100	8,000
NATO	12,800	–	8,400	420	650	1,400	–	290	–	575	–	1,100
WARSAW PACT	11,300	6,700	–	70	10	–	2,700	–	1,500	–	30	290
OPEC**	35,600	13,100	9,000	3,500	2,000	2,000	360	1,300	250	260	950	2,800
AFRICA	21,500	11,300	825	2,400	360	1,400	340	1,200	280	60	330	3,000
ALGERIA**	2,300	1,800	–	–	20	370	–	10	–	–	–	90
ANGOLA	950	550	–	10	10	10	20	–	50	5	40	260
BENIN	30	20	–	–	–	–	–	–	–	–	–	10
BOTSWANA	20	–	–	–	20	–	–	–	–	–	–	5
BURUNDI	20	10	–	–	–	–	–	–	–	–	–	5
CAMEROON	20	–	20	–	–	–	–	–	–	–	–	5
CAPE VERDE	50	50	–	–	–	–	–	–	–	–	–	–
CENTRAL AFRICAN REP	10	–	–	5	–	–	–	–	–	–	–	10
CHAD	10	5	–	–	–	–	–	–	–	–	–	–
CONGO	70	60	–	5	–	–	–	–	–	–	–	–
EQUATORIAL GUINEA	20	10	–	–	–	–	–	–	–	–	–	5
ETHIOPIA	2,300	1,900	80	10	–	5	40	–	10	–	10	140
GABON**	110	–	5	60	–	–	–	30	–	–	–	30
GAMBIA	5	–	–	–	–	–	–	10	–	–	–	5
GHANA	130	–	–	–	5	50	–	20	–	40	–	20
GUINEA-BISSAU	30	30	–	–	–	–	–	–	–	–	–	–

Country											
GUINEA	50	50	–	–	–	–	–	–	–	–	–
IVORY COAST	250	–	200	–	–	–	–	–	–	–	50
KENYA	180	–	30	40	–	–	–	–	20	–	40
LESOTHO	–	–	–	–	–	–	–	–	–	–	–
LIBERIA	10	–	410	50	460	280	575	220	–	230	5
LIBYA**	8,600	5,500	–	–	–	–	–	–	–	–	850
MADAGASCAR	80	60	10	10	5	–	–	–	–	–	10
MALAWI	30	–	10	–	–	–	–	–	–	–	5
MALI	120	110	–	–	10	–	–	–	–	–	5
MAURITANIA	90	–	40	–	–	–	–	–	–	–	50
MAURITIUS	–	–	–	–	50	5	50	–	–	–	–
MOROCCO	2,000	5	380	1,100	50	–	–	–	–	–	390
MOZAMBIQUE	280	180	40	–	10	–	–	–	–	–	90
NIGER	40	–	50	110	50	–	–	–	–	–	–
NIGERIA**	330	90	–	–	–	–	–	–	–	–	5
RWANDA	30	–	–	–	–	–	–	–	–	–	30
SAO TOME & PRINCIPE	–	–	–	–	–	–	–	–	–	–	–
SENEGAL	70	–	30	–	10	–	–	–	–	–	40
SIERRA LEONE	5	150	–	10	–	–	–	–	–	–	–
SOMALIA	750	–	40	–	10	–	340	–	–	–	200
SOUTH AFRICA*	460	20	200	–	–	–	40	–	–	–	210
SUDAN	575	140	5	–	360	–	–	–	–	10	50
SWAZILAND	–	–	–	–	–	–	–	–	–	–	–
TANZANIA	470	320	5	10	–	–	5	–	–	10	120
TOGO	40	–	20	10	5	5	–	–	–	–	20
TUNISIA	220	60	10	5	20	–	40	–	–	5	80
UGANDA	60	–	–	5	–	–	–	–	–	5	–
UPPER VOLTA	30	40	110	5	10	–	–	–	–	–	10
ZAIRE	240	–	–	20	5	–	20	–	–	–	70
ZAMBIA	340	220	–	40	5	–	20	–	–	20	60
ZIMBABWE	90	–	–	–	–	–	–	–	–	–	50

– None or negligible.   * Developed country.   ** OPEC country.

Note:

To avoid the appearance of excessive accuracy, all numbers in this table are independently rounded, with greater severity for larger numbers. Therefore, components may not add to totals.

Table 5. Number of Arms Delivered, Cumulative 1976–1980, by Selected Supplier,[a] Recipient Developing Region,[b] and Major Weapon Type

SUPPLIER / EQUIPMENT TYPE	TOTAL	SOVIET UNION	OTHER WARSAW PACT	UNITED STATES[c]	FRANCE	UNITED KINGDOM	OTHER NATO	CHINA
ALL DEVELOPING RECIPIENTS[b]								
LAND ARMAMENTS								
TANKS	13,425	6,850	2,480	2,295	280	695	95	730
ANTI-AIR ARTILLERY[d]	7,175	3,150	900	1,895	100	130	370	630
FIELD ARTILLERY[e]	10,890	5,485	430	3,430	410	90	555	490
ARMORED PERSONNEL CARRIERS	21,405	9,005	240	8,745	2,440	265	705	5
NAVAL CRAFT								
MAJOR SURFACE COMBATANTS[f]	109	27	9	29	14	12	18	–
OTHER SURFACE COMBATANTS[g]	481	116	5	152	50	51	83	24
SUBMARINES	24	6	–	3	2	7	6	–
MISSILE ATTACK BOATS	74	56	–	–	10	–	8	–
AIRCRAFT								
COMBAT AIRCRAFT: SUPERSONIC	3,600	2,120	–	915	250	40	–	275
COMBAT AIRCRAFT: SUBSONIC	790	335	–	395	35	15	–	10
OTHER AIRCRAFT[h]	1,805	310	230	435	95	170	385	180
HELICOPTERS	2,380	810	65	425	680	30	360	10
MISSILES								
SURFACE TO AIR	25,215	15,040	200	8,030	550	1,395	–	–

AFRICA

LAND ARMAMENTS								
TANKS	3,250	2,010	1,100	-	10	55	-	65
ANTI-AIR ARTILLERY[d]	2,310	1,520	140	275	10	25	105	235
FIELD ARTILLERY[e]	3,940	2,635	410	50	320	45	215	265
ARMORED PERSONNEL CARRIERS	5,110	3,245	100	5	1,155	100	505	-
NAVAL CRAFT								
MAJOR SURFACE COMBATANTS[f]	29	7	4	-	9	2	7	-
OTHER SURFACE COMBATANTS[g]	133	45	-	-	43	8	29	8
SUBMARINES	3	3	-	-	-	-	-	-
MISSILE ATTACK BOATS	23	22	-	-	1	-	-	-
AIRCRAFT								
COMBAT AIRCRAFT: SUPERSONIC	930	770	-	20	100	-	-	40
COMBAT AIRCRAFT: SUBSONIC	150	115	85	-	35	5	-	-
OTHER AIRCRAFT[h]	495	85	40	10	25	55	225	10
HELICOPTERS	520	215	-	5	110	-	140	10
MISSILES								
SURFACE TO AIR	5,600	5,390	200	-	-	10	-	-

[a] The suppliers included are the five largest single exporters of major weapons in terms of magnitude of deliveries as well as other countries of the two major alliances.

[b] Totals include the "developing" countries, as previously listed, with the exception of Albania, Greece, Malta, Spain, Turkey and Yugoslavia.

[c] U.S. data are by fiscal years 1976–1980, while other suppliers' data are by calendar years 1976–1980.

[d] Air defense artillery includes weapons over 23 mm.

[e] Field artillery includes mobile rocket launchers, mortars, and recoilless rifles over 100 mm.

[f] Major surface combatants include aircraft carriers, cruisers, destroyers, destroyer escorts, and frigates.

[g] Minor surface combatants include motor torpedo boats, subchasers and minesweepers.

[h] Other aircraft include reconnaissance aircraft, trainers, transports and utility aircraft.

Notes

Chapter 1

1. Leonard Binder et al., *Crises and Sequences in Political Development* (Princeton: Princeton University Press, 1971), p. 35.

2. Dudley Seers, "Challenges to Development Theory and Strategy: The Meaning of Development," *International Development Review* 4 (December 1969), pp. 2–6.

3. UNESCO, *Yearbook on Peace and Conflict Studies* (Westport, CT: Greenwood Press, 1981), p. 222.

4. See Bruce E. Arlinghaus, "Social versus Military Development: Positive and Normative Dimensions," in James E. Katz, ed., *Arms Production and Trade in Developing Countries: An Analysis of Decision-Making* (Lexington, MA: D. C. Heath, 1983).

5. Elmo R. Zumwalt, Jr., "America's Naval Strategy Has Been Made Obsolete by Technology," *Los Angeles Times*, August 9, 1981, p. 2E.

6. Thomas Powers, "Choosing a Strategy for World War III," *Atlantic* 250, no. 5 (November 1982), pp. 82–110.

7. Glenn H. Snyder, *Deterrence and Defense: Toward a Theory of National Security* (Princeton: Princeton University Press, 1961).

8. Frank N. Trager and Frank L. Simonie, "An Introduction to the Study of National Security," in F. Trager and P. Kronenburg, eds., *National Security and American Policy* (Lawrence: University of Kansas Press, 1973), pp. 35–48.

9. Amos A. Jordan, William J. Taylor, Jr., and Associates, *American National Security: Policy and Process* (Baltimore: Johns Hopkins University Press, 1981), pp. 2–3.

10. Ernest W. Lefever, *Spear and Scepter: Army, Police, and Politics in Tropical Africa* (Washington, D.C.: Brookings Institution, 1970), p. 20.

11. Jonathan Schell, *The Fate of the Earth* (New York: Avon, 1982), p. 186. For a more far-ranging analysis (though woefully short of African data), see William H. McNeill, *The Pursuit of Power: Technology, Armed Force, and Society Since AD 1000* (Chicago: University of Chicago Press, 1982).

12. Quoted in Kenneth L. Adelman, "African Security: Facts and Fantasies," *Comparative Strategy* 2, no. 1 (Spring 1980), pp. 97–108.

13. Lawrence Baraebibai Ekpebu, "An African Perspective on US/USSR/China Arms Policies," *Alternatives* 6, no. 1 (March 1980), pp. 93–129.

14. Thomas M. Callaghy, "The Rise of the African State," *Problems of Communism*, September–October 1980, pp. 54–60.

15. I. William Zartman, "Issues of African Diplomacy in the 1980s," *Orbis* 25, no. 4 (Winter 1982), pp. 1025–1043.

16. Richard E. Bissell, "The Pursuit of Coherence," *Orbis* 25, no. 4 (Winter 1982), pp. 853–855.

17. Robert S. McNamara, *The Essence of Security* (New York: Harper and Row, 1968), p. 149.

18. Stephanie G. Neuman, "The Positive Effects of Arms Transfers," *New York Times*, June 10, 1977.

19. Compare Herman Kahn, *World Economic Development 1979 and Beyond* (Boulder, CO: Westview Press, 1979), pp. 463–465, with Henry A. Kissinger, *The White House Years* (Boston: Little, Brown, 1979), p. 1260. Also see Avi Plascov, *Security in the Persian Gulf: Modernization, Political Development, and Stability* (London: International Institute for Strategic Studies, 1982), p. 109.

20. Steven P. Cohen, "Toward a Great State in Asia?" in O. Marwah and J. D. Pollack, eds., *Military Power and Policy in Asian States: China, India, Japan* (Boulder, CO: Westview Press, 1980), p. 11.

21. Jan Pettman, *Zambia: Security and Conflict* (London: Julian Friedman, 1974).

22. John M. Ostheimer and Gary J. Buckley, "Nigeria," in E. Kolodziej and R. Harkavy, eds., *Security Policies of Developing Nations* (Lexington, MA: D. C. Heath 1982), pp. 285–303. For a comparison, see Samora Machel's speech reported in Foreign Broadcast Information Service, *Subsaharan Africa*, November 18, 1981, p. U1. In it, he stresses defense of national sovereignty, territorial integrity, national unity ("Our armed forces are the highest expression of the unity of the Mozambique people"), defense of the revolution, and the building of socialism. Apparently his army is one such as he claims, engaged in production and composed of armed politicians and workers.

23. Peter B. Riddleberger, *Military Roles in Developing Countries: An Inventory of Past Research and Analysis* (Washington, D.C.: American University, 1965).

24. See Stephanie Neuman and Robert Harkavy, eds., *Defense Planning in Less-Industrialized Countries* (Lexington, MA: D. C. Heath, 1983), and Douglas J. Murray and Paul R. Viotti, eds., *The Defense Policies of Nations: A Comparative Study* (Baltimore: Johns Hopkins University Press, 1982), pp. 5–7.

25. John M. Collins, *U.S. Defense Planning: A Critique* (Boulder, CO: Westview Press, 1982), pp. 3–8.

26. Department of Army, *FM-100-5: Operations* (Washington, D.C.: U.S. Government Printing Office, 1982), pp. 2–3.

27. Lawrence J. Korb, Jr., assistant secretary of defense for manpower, reserve affairs, and logistics (speech at the Georgetown University Center for Strategic and International Studies, Washington, D.C., January 17, 1983).

28. Walter L. Barrows, "Changing Military Capabilities in Sub-Saharan Africa," in Henry S. Bienen and William J. Foltz, eds., *Arms and the African: The Militarization of African Interstate Relations* (New Haven, CT: Yale University Press, 1983).

29. Edward A. Kolodziej and Robert Harkavy, "Developing States and the International Security System," *Journal of International Affairs* 34, no. 1 (Spring–Summer 1980), pp. 59–87.

30. Geoffrey Kemp, "U.S. Strategic Interests and Military Options in Sub-Saharan Africa," in Jennifer S. Whittaker, ed., *Africa and the United States: Vital Interests* (New York: New York University Press, 1978).

31. Harold A. Hovey, *United States Military Assistance: A Study of Policies and Practices* (New York: Praeger, 1965), p. 109.

32. Stephanie Neuman, "Security, Military Expenditures, and Socioeconomic Development: Reflections on Iran," *Orbis* 22, no. 3 (Fall 1978), p. 583.

33. Peter B. Riddleberger, *Military Roles in Developing Countries*; John J. Johnson, ed., *The Role of the Military in Underdeveloped Countries* (Princeton: Princeton University Press, 1962); and Cyril E. Black, "Military Leadership and National Development," in D. MacIssac, ed., *The Military and Society* (Colorado Springs: U.S. Air Force Academy, 1972), pp. 16–35. Not surprisingly, many African leaders also share this perception. Reportedly, Nimeiry of Sudan believes that his army is the most disciplined organization in the country (it certainly is one of the best disciplined armies in Africa), and he recommends military rule for Africa and those nations torn by tribalism. See Alan Cowell, "Egypt's Friend in Need," *New York Times Magazine*, December 20, 1981, pp. 38–68.

34. Lefever, *Spear and Scepter*, p. 20.

35. David Carney, "Notes on Disarmament and African Development," in Fredrick S. Arkhurst, ed., *Arms and African Development* (New York: Praeger, 1970), pp. 23–30.

36. Claude E. Welch, Jr., "The African Military and Political Development," in Henry Bienen, ed., *The Military and Modernization* (Chicago: Atherton, 1971), pp. 212–233.

37. Eric A. Nordlinger, "Soldiers in Mufti: The Impact of Military Rule Upon Economic and Social Change in the Non-Western States," *American Political Science Review* 64 (1970), pp. 1131–1148.

38. See Welch, "The African Military," and Morris L. Janowitz, *Military Institutions and Coercion in the Developing Nations* (Chicago: University of Chicago Press, 1977), p. 110.

39. Sam C. Sarkesian, "African Military Regimes: Institutionalized Instability or Coercive Development," in Sheldon W. Simon, ed., *The Military and Security in the Third World: Domestic and International Impacts* (Boulder, CO: Westview Press, 1978), pp. 15–46.

40. Emile Benoit, *Defense and Economic Growth in Developing Countries* (Lexington, MA: D. C. Heath, 1973), p. 3.

41. Nicole Ball, "Defense and Development: A Critique of the Benoit Study," *Economic Development and Cultural Change* 31, no. 3 (April 1983), pp. 507–524.

42. R. D. McKinley and A. S. Cohen, "The Economic Performance of Military Regimes: A Cross-National Aggregate Study," *British Journal of Political Science* (July 1976), pp. 291–310.

43. Emile Benoit, "Growth and Defense in Developing Countries," *World Politics* 26, no. 3 (April 1977), pp. 271–280.

44. Peter C. Fredrickson and Robert E. Looney, "Defense Expenditures and Economic Growth in Developing Countries: Some Further Empirical Evidence" (U.S. Naval Postgraduate School, Monterey, CA, 1982, mimeo).

45. Nordlinger, "Soldiers in Mufti," and Robin Luckham, The Nigerian Military: A Sociological Analysis of Authority and Revolt 1960–67 (Cambridge: Cambridge University Press, 1971), p. 94.

46. Harry F. Waterhouse, A Time to Build: Military Civic Action, Medium for Economic Development and Social Reform (Columbia: University of South Carolina Press, 1964); Hugh Hanning, The Peaceful Uses of Military Forces (New York: Praeger, 1967); and H. R. Heitman, "The Potential Role of the Military in National Development," Militaria, February 8, 1978, pp. 1–11.

47. Lucian W. Pye, "Armies in the Process of Political Modernization," in Johnson, The Role of the Military, p. 82.

48. Eric A. Nordlinger, Soldiers in Politics: Military Coups and Governments (Englewood Cliffs, NJ: Prentice-Hall, 1977), p. 168.

49. Rolland G. Paulston, Planning Non-Formal Educational Alternatives: National Youth Service Organizations in the Less Developed Countries, SEADAG Papers no. 72-4 (New York: The Asia Society, 1972). Also see Sabi H. Shabtai, "Army and Economy in Tropical Africa," Economic Development and Cultural Change 23, no. 4 (June 1975), pp. 687–701, and Jorgen Rask Hansen, "Botswana: The Brigade's Controversy," Africa Report 27, no. 6 (November–December 1982), pp. 54–56.

50. U.S. Department of State, Liberia: The Road to Recovery, Current Policy no. 343 (Washington, D.C.: U.S. Government Printing Office, 1981), p. 4.

51. Chemist Mafuba, "Army to Help Move Maize," Herald (Salisbury), July 31, 1981, p. 13.

52. Tony Avirgan and Martha Honey, War in Uganda: The Legacy of Idi Amin (Westport, CT: Lawrence Hill and Co., 1982), pp. 53–70. Julius Nyerere's position on the military is well known. In Freedom and Development: A Selection from Writings and Speeches 1968–1973 (Dar es Salaam: Oxford University Press, 1973) he said, "The National Service is, in fact, basically not a military force at all. Its job is to make a contribution to the development of our economy. . . . " And it was not to be confused with professional soldiers, whom he saw as nation builders, also. He was quoted as saying, "Here are these able-bodied men, why can't they help build bridges?" in David K. Whynes, The Economics of Third World Military Expenditure (Austin: University of Texas Press, 1979), p. 137.

53. Issac Mruma, "Parliament Debates JKU Merger, Defense Estimates," Dar es Salaam Daily News, July 24, 1981, p. 1, and Mkumbwa Ally, "Minister Says Civil Defence Body Planned," Dar es Salaam Daily News, July 24, 1981, p. 1.

54. Mary Kaldor and Absjorn Eide, eds., The World Military Order: The Impact of Military Technology in the Third World (New York: Praeger, 1979), pp. 2–3.

55. See Mary Kaldor, "The Military in Development," World Development 4, no. 6 (June 1976), pp. 459–482, and Absjorn Eide and Marek Thee, eds., Problems of Contemporary Militarism (New York: St. Martin's Press, 1980).

56. Richard Jolly, ed., Disarmament and World Development (New York: Pergamon, 1978), especially essays by Luckham and Kaldor.

57. See Roger Murray, "Militarism in Africa," *New Left Review*, no. 38 (July–August 1966), and Robin Luckham, "Armaments, Underdevelopment, and De-militarization in Africa," *Alternatives* 6, no. 3 (September 1980), pp. 179–245.

58. William F. Gutteridge, "The Political Role of African Armed Forces: The Impact of Foreign Military Assistance," *African Affairs* 66, no. 1 (April 1967), pp. 93–101; Edward T. Rowe, "Aid and Coups d'Etat: Aspects of the Impact of American Military Assistance Programs in the Less Developed Countries," *International Studies Quarterly* 18, no. 2 (June 1974), pp. 239–255; and Ilan Peleg, "Arms Supply to the Third World—Models and Explanations," *Journal of Modern African Studies* 5, no. 1 (1977), pp. 91–103.

59. For an early discussion of this issue, see Col. David R. Hughes, "The Myth of Military Coups and Military Assistance," *Military Review* 47, no. 12 (December 1967), pp. 3–10.

60. See Ruth Leger Sivard, *World Military and Social Expenditures 1981* (Leesburg, VA: World Priorities, 1981), p. 7.

61. Alan Cowell, "Zaire Army Guards Key Kinshasa Sites," *New York Times*, August 9, 1981, and "Zaire: The Squeeze Hurts," *Economist*, October 17, 1981, p. 40.

62. Henry S. Bienen, "Military Rule and Military Order in Africa," *Orbis* 25, no. 4 (Winter 1982), pp. 949–965.

63. Amos Perlmutter, "The Comparative Analysis of Military Regimes: For-mations, Aspirations, and Achievements," *World Politics* 33, no. 1 (October 1980), pp. 96–120.

64. See Walter L. Barrows, "Dynamics of Military Rule in Black Africa" (paper presented at the National Defense University, Washington, D.C., September 1982, mimeo), and the essays in Issac James Mowoe, ed., *The Performance of Soldiers as Governors: African Politics and the African Military* (Washington, D.C.: University Press of America, 1980).

65. Stanislav Andreski, "On the Peaceful Disposition of Military Dictator-ships," *Journal of Strategic Studies* (1980).

66. Kenneth Fidel, ed., *Militarism in Developing Countries* (Rutgers, NJ: Transaction Books, 1975), p. 11, and Robert I. Rotberg, "After Ghana—More Coups in Africa?" *Christian Science Monitor*, January 20, 1982.

67. David D. Laitin and Drew A. Harker, "Military Rule and National Secession: Nigeria and Ethiopia," in Morris Janowitz, ed., *Civil-Military Relations: Regional Perspectives* (New York: Sage, 1982).

68. Victor A. Olorunsola, *Soldiers and Power: The Development Performance of the Nigerian Military Regime* (Stanford, CA: Hoover Institution Press, 1977), and Olatunde Odetola, *Military Regimes and Development: A Comparative Analysis in African Societies* (London: Allen and Unwin, 1982).

69. Dennis Austin, *Politics in Africa* (Hanover, NH: University of New England Press, 1978), p. 54. Also see Sarkesian, "African Military Regimes."

70. James V. D'Amato and Elizabeth D. Thompson, "After the Coup: Increasing Level of Militarization in African Countries?" (paper read at the annual meetings of the International Studies Association, Cincinnati, OH, March 1982, mimeo).

71. Raymond W. Copson, "African Flashpoints: Prospects for Armed Inter-national Conflict," *Orbis* 25, no. 4 (Winter 1982), pp. 903–923.

72. See Richard H. Deutsch, "Fueling the African Arms Race," *Africa Report* 22 (March–April 1977), pp. 50–52, and Richard H. Deutsch, "Africa's Arms Race," *Africa Report* 24 (March–April 1979), pp. 47–49. Also see "Arms in the Ocean," *South*, November 1980, pp. 19–20.

73. For an excellent summary of the relevant portions of the Brandt report, see Olof Palme et al., "Military Spending: The Economic and Social Consequences," *Challenge* 25, no. 4 (September/October 1982), pp. 4–21. See also Raimo Vayrynen, "Economic and Political Consequences of Arms Transfers to the Third World," *Alternatives* 6, no. 1 (March 1980), pp. 131–155, and Peter Lock, "Armaments Dynamics: An Issue in Development Strategies," *Alternatives* 6, no. 2 (July 1980), pp. 157–178. The Soviets are not ignorant of the propaganda value of such concerns, and in a recent book that "shows the consistent struggle of the USSR and other socialist countries, of all progressive forces, for stopping the arms race and for disarmament," there is no mention of the level of Soviet arms supplies to the Third World. See R. Faramazyan, *Disarmament and the Economy* (Moscow: Progress Publishers, 1981).

74. For discussions of the UN in this area see Inga Thorsson, "Study on Disarmament and Development," *Bulletin of the Atomic Scientists* 38 (June/July 1982), pp. 41–44, and Nicole Ball, "Military Expenditures in the Development Process: An Overview" (paper read at the annual meetings of the International Studies Association, Cincinnati, OH, March 1982). Examples of the research reports commissioned by the UN Group of Governmental Experts on the Relationship between Disarmament and Development include Dan Smith and Ron Smith, "Military Expenditure, Resources, and Development" (University of London, 1980, mimeo), and Bruce M. Russett and David J. Sylvan, "The Effects of Arms Transfers on Developing Countries" (Yale University, 1980, mimeo). Since those arguing that military expenditures *aid* development cannot provide conclusive data to support their position, the more intuitive argument that such expenditures retard development appears to win out, even though the data are no more conclusive.

75. *United Nations Disarmament Yearbook*, vol. 3 (New York: United Nations, 1978) p. 401.

76. Arkhurst, *Arms and African Development*, p. 19.

77. See "The New Defense Posture: Missiles, Missiles, and Missiles," *Business Week*, August 11, 1980, pp. 76–81; Robert Kennedy, "Precision ATGMs and NATO Defense," *Orbis* 22, no. 4 (Winter 1979), pp. 897–927; and Drew Middleton, "U.S. Is Relying on Sleek New Arms," *New York Times*, March 23, 1981, p. A11.

78. Paul F. Walker, "Precision-Guided Munitions," *Scientific American* 245, no. 2 (August 1981), pp. 37–45, and "Smart Weapons in Naval Warfare," *Scientific American* 248, no. 5 (May 1983), pp. 53–61.

79. See the essays in Geoffrey A. Kemp, Robert L. Pfaltzgraff, Jr., and Uri Ra'anan, eds., *The Other Arms Race: New Technologies and Non-Nuclear Conflict* (Lexington, MA: D. C. Heath, 1975).

80. Mary Kaldor, *The Baroque Arsenal* (New York: Hill and Wang, 1981), p. 173.

81. Adam Roberts, *Nation in Arms: The Theory and Practice of Territorial Defense* (New York: Praeger, 1976), p. 259. For a detailed example of an alternative military system, see Herbert Wulf, "Dependent Militarism in the Periphery and Possible Alternative Concepts," in Stephanie Neuman and Robert Harkavy, eds., *Arms Transfers in the Modern World* (New York: Praeger, 1978), pp. 246–263. In this essay, Wulf contrasts conventional "technocratic" armies with people's militias. The former are seen as costly, specialized, capital-intensive institutions that require numerous foreign technicians, alliances, and professional standing armies and are subordinated to rigid military command structures bent on military expansionism. The latter are contrasted as inexpensive, diverse, labor-intensive organizations armed with simple weapons not requiring foreign support. These militias support a policy of nonalignment and defensive neutralism, based upon social mobilization during times of war, under democratic, decentralized control. During peacetime, the only mobilization would be for training purposes.

82. See Bruce E. Arlinghaus, "Smart Bombs and Dumb Soldiers: Precision-Guided Munitions and the All-Volunteer Force," in William J. Taylor, Jr., Eric T. Olsen, and Richard A. Schrader, eds., *Defense Manpower Planning: Issues for the 1980s* (New York: Pergamon, 1981), pp. 80–87.

83. Government Accounting Office, *Implications of Highly Sophisticated Weapon Systems on Military Capabilities* (Washington, D.C.: U.S. Government Printing Office, 1980), Report no. PSAD-80-61.

84. Drew Middleton, *Can America Win the Next War?* (New York: Scribner's, 1975), p. 104; James Fallows, *National Defense* (New York: Random House, 1981), pp. 38–63; "The Trap of Rearmament," *New York Review*, December 17, 1981, pp. 26–31; Frank Greve, "Dream Weapon a Nightmare," *Philadelphia Inquirer*, May 2, 1982; and Gregg Easterbrook, "DIVAD," *Atlantic Monthly* (October 1982), pp. 29–39, who states, "The most sophisticated weapon ever to roll onto a battlefield is a treat for contractors but a liability for soldiers in battle."

85. See George C. Wilson and William J. Perry, "Are Our Weapons Too Complex? Not If You Compare Them to the Russians," *Washington Post*, February 22, 1981, pp. C1–C5; "High-cost Lemons in the U.S. Arsenal," *Science* 212, (April 17, 1981), pp. 309–310, 312; James Coates, "Defense Analyst Blasts Decline in Weapons," *Chicago Tribune*, March 15, 1981, p. 1; "Defence: Bring Out the Guard," *Economist*, May 1, 1982, p. 31; "Defence: Tackled on Television," *Economist*, June 13, 1981, pp. 25–26; "Arming for the 1980s," *Time*, July 27, 1981, pp. 6–21; "Fighting to Win the War," *Newsweek*, September 14, 1981, p. 27; and "Where to Cut Defense," *Newsweek*, December 20, 1982, pp. 24–31.

Chapter 2

1. David K. Whynes, *The Economics of Third World Military Expenditure* (Austin: University of Texas Press, 1979), p. 54. The fourth stage of this evolution is the acquisition of nuclear weapons, but only Libya and South Africa in the region are believed to have reached this stage.

2. William J. Foltz, "Arms and the African: Trends and Policy Problems for the 1980s," Background Paper no. 5 (Study Group on Military Factors in African Politics, Council on Foreign Relations, New York, 1980, mimeo), pp. 4–8.

3. Daniel Volman, *A Continent Besieged: Foreign Military Activities in Africa Since 1975* (Washington, D.C.: Institute for Policy Studies, n.d.), p. 1.

4. Based on A.G.G. Gimjena-Pineywa and Ali A. Mazrui, "Regional Development: African Perspectives," in Fredrick Arkhurst, ed., *Arms and African Development* (New York: Praeger, 1970), pp. 31–45, and Ali A. Mazrui, *Africa's International Relations: The Diplomacy of Dependency and Change* (Boulder, CO: Westview Press, 1977), pp. 235–237.

5. J. 'Bayo Adekson, *Nigeria in Search of a Stable Civil-Military System* (Boulder, CO: Westview Press, 1981), and Cynthia H. Enloe, *Police, Military, and Ethnicity: Foundations of State Power* (New Brunswick, NJ: Transaction Books, 1980), p. 41.

6. Rene Lemarchand, "African Armies in Historical and Contemporary Perspectives: The Search for Connections," *Journal of Political and Military Sociology* 10, no. 2 (Fall 1981), and S. Ukpabi, "Military Considerations in African Foreign Policies," *Transition* 6, no. 31 (June/July 1967), pp. 35–40.

7. Ali A. Mazrui, *Soldiers and Kinsmen in Uganda: The Making of a Military Ethnocracy* (Beverly Hills, CA: Sage, 1975), pp. 55–56, 278.

8. See J. M. Lee, *African Armies and the Civil Order* (London: Chatto and Windus, 1969); Martin Kilson, "Politics of the African Military," *Armed Forces and Society* 2, no. 2 (Winter 1976), pp. 333–336; Sam DeCalo, *Coups and Army Rule in Africa* (New Haven, CT: Yale University Press, 1976); and Robert H. Jackson and Carl A. Rosberg, *Personal Rule in Black Africa* (Berkeley: University of California Press, 1982).

9. Enloe, *Police, Military and Ethnicity*, pp. 35–37.

10. This short summary was based upon William F. Gutteridge, "Military and Police Forces in Colonial Africa," in L. H. Gann and Peter Duignan, eds., *Colonialism in Africa, 1870–1960, vol. 2, The History and Politics of Colonialism, 1914–1960* (Cambridge: Cambridge University Press, 1970), pp. 286–319, and William F. Gutteridge, *Military Regimes in Africa* (London: Methuen, 1975), pp. 31–53. For the effects of overseas service during the world wars, see Rita Headrick, "African Soldiers in World War II," *Armed Forces and Society* 4, no. 4 (Summer 1978), pp. 501–526. It is interesting to note that only Tanzania, Sierra Leone, and Gambia seriously questioned the need for professional armed forces and that virtually all African armed forces are based upon volunteer service rather than conscription.

11. Seth Singleton, "Supplementary Military Forces in SubSaharan Africa: The Congo, Kenya, Tanzania, Uganda, and Zaire," in Louis A. Zucker and Gwyn Harries Jenkins, eds., *Supplementary Military Forces* (Beverly Hills, CA: Sage, 1978), pp. 200–237.

12. Henry Bienen, *Armies and Parties in Africa* (New York: Africana Publishing Co., 1978), p. 100.

13. Chester A. Crocker, "Military Dependence: The Colonial Legacy in Africa," *Journal of Modern African Studies* 12 (June 1974), pp. 265–286.

14. See *The World Military Balance, 1982–1983,* (London: International Institute for Strategic Studies, 1982), p. 65, for a listing of such agreements.

15. J. F. Maitland Jones, *Politics in Africa: The Former British Territories* (New York: Norton, 1975), pp. 110–129; Akiwowo Akinsola, "The Armed Forces in

the Nigerian Economy: A Sociologist's Approach," *Politico* 37, no. 3 (September 1972), pp. 562–581; and Bienen, *Armies and Parties*, p. 112.

16. John Worrall, "Uganda's Leader's Key Problem May Be His Own Army," *Christian Science Monitor*, November 24, 1981, and "Mobutu Endures as Symbol and Pervasive Force," *New York Times*, August 18, 1981, p. A2.

17. See Raymond W. Copson, "African International Politics: Underdevelopment and Conflict in the Seventies," *Orbis* 22, no. 1 (Spring 1978), pp. 227–245; Ada A. Bozeman, *Conflict in Africa: Concepts and Realities* (Princeton: Princeton University Press, 1976); and Melvin Small and J. David Singer, *Resort To Arms: International and Civil Wars, 1816–1980* (Beverly Hills, CA: Sage, 1982).

18. Colin Legum et al., *Africa in the 1980s* (New York: McGraw-Hill, 1979), p. 45.

19. Africa has some 48 nations with 105 common boundaries. See Ian Brownlie, *African Boundaries: A Legal and Diplomatic Encyclopedia* (Los Angeles: University of California Press, 1979). For recent examples, see "Clashes in Gabon," *Africa*, no. 119 (July 1981), p. 10, and "Nigeria and Cameroon: To Hell with Unity," *Economist*, June 6, 1981, p. 52.

20. "Ethiopia: Is a Nod as Good as a Wink?" *Economist*, June 6, 1981, pp. 51–52.

21. Quoted in Anthony Lewis, "Vision and Reality," *New York Times*, January 24, 1983, p. A19.

22. See "Black Gold," *Economist*, December 5, 1981, p. 86, and Robert J. Lilley, "Restraints on Superpower Intervention in Sub-Saharan Africa," *Parameters* 12, no. 3 (September 1982), pp. 63–75.

23. Quoted in Ray Moseley, "For Many Millions, Empty Hopes and Empty Bellies," *Chicago Tribune*, September 28, 1981. Also see "Where Natural and Man-Made Disasters Get Together," *Economist*, June 14, 1980, pp. 37–38; "The Killer in the Aid Bag," *Economist*, December 26, 1981, pp. 79–81; and Yohannis Abate, "Population Growth and Urbanization in Africa," *Current History* 78, no. 455 (March 1980), pp. 102–106, 132–133.

24. Victor T. Levine, "Problems of Political Succession in Independent Africa," in Ali A. Mazrui and Hasu H. Patel, eds., *Africa in World Affairs: The Next Thirty Years* (New York: Third Press, 1973), pp. 79–103; Lancine Sylla, "Succession of the Charismatic Leader: The Gordian Knot of African Politics," *Daedalus* 136 (Spring 1982), pp. 11–28; and "Cameroon: African Country Changes Ruler Without a Coup," *Economist*, November 13, 1982, pp. 92–94.

25. Antero Pietila, "Transkei Plans to Draft Army Out of Fear of Black Nationalism," *Chicago Sun*, October 6, 1981; "Unidentified Raiders Attack Principal Zimbabwe Air Base," *New York Times*, July 26, 1982, p. A3; and John Kraus, "Islamic Affinities and International Politics in Sub-Saharan Africa," *Current History* 78, no. 456 (April 1980), pp. 154–158, 182–184.

26. Stephen Taylor, "Officers Given Credit for Holding Troops Together," *Times* (London), June 21, 1982; "Zimbabwe Molds 3 Warring Forces Into Single Army," *Chicago Sun*, March 22, 1981; Paul Van Slambouck, "Zimbabwe To Cut Army Size, But Will Soldiers Stay Calm?" *Christian Science Monitor*, February 23, 1982, p. 4; "Zimbabwe Strives to Cut Its Forces," *New York Times*, October

8, 1981; and "Zimbabwe: Shots From the Hip," *Economist*, September 19, 1981, pp. 44–45.

27. "OAU Assembly XVIII," *African Index* 4, no. 11 (July 15, 1981), p. 43; *The Organisation of African Unity: A Role for the 1980s*, Report no. 10 (New York: International Peace Academy, 1980); and Nosakare O. Obaseki, *Managing Africa's Conflicts*, Report no. 12 (New York: International Peace Academy, 1982).

28. B. David Meyers, "An Analysis of the OAU's Effectiveness at Regional Collective Defense," in Yassin El-Aouty, ed., *The Organization of African Unity After Ten Years* (New York: Praeger, 1975), pp. 118–134, and John Ostheimer, "African Defense and Economic Cooperation" in Bruce E. Arlinghaus, ed., *African Security Issues: Sovereignty, Stability, and Solidarity* (Boulder, CO: Westview Press, 1984).

29. For a recent example in Chad, see: Thomas J. Wertso, "The Organization of African Unity and Peacekeeping in Africa" (paper read at the annual meetings of the African Studies Association, Washington, D.C., 1982, mimeo); "What African Unity?" *Economist*, March 13, 1982, pp. 14–15; Michael Collins Dunn, "Chad: The OAU Tries Peacekeeping," *Washington Quarterly* 5, no. 2 (Spring 1982), pp. 182–188; "France and Chad: Army vs. Army vs. Army," *Economist*, October 31, 1981, p. 49; W. F. Gutteridge, "The OAU Peace Force: Fighting to Survive?" *New African*, no. 174 (March 1982), p. 40; Don Oberdorfer, "Mobutu, in Talks Here, Seeks More Military Aid," *Washington Post*, December 1, 1981; "Chad: So Simple," *Economist*, February 20, 1982, pp. 60–61; Bernard DeGiovanni, "Rebel Forces, After Short Fight, Overthrow Government of Chad," *Washington Post*, June 8, 1982, p. A14. Perhaps the most succinct summary of the experience of the first Inter-African Peacekeeping Force was one diplomat's comment: "Unfortunately, those groups are often better at looting than at keeping peace." Quoted in Frank J. Prial, "France Seeking Closer African Ties," *New York Times*, September 28, 1981, p. A3. The irony of this comment is that African participation in UN peacekeeping forces (by Ghana, Liberia, Morocco, Nigeria, Senegal, Sierra Leone, and Tunisia) has been very successful, both as a training experience and in actual performance of duties. See Edward B. Davis and Sheila M. Davis, "Small Armies and United Nations Peacekeeping Operations" (paper read at the annual meetings of the International Studies Association, Cincinnati, OH, March 1982, mimeo).

30. Hugh Hanning, "Lifebelt For Africa: The OAU in the 1980s," *The World Today* (July–August 1981), pp. 311–316. On an African high command, see B.I.C. Ijomah, "The Rationale for an African Military High Command," *Armed Forces and Society* 3, no. 4 (August 1977), pp. 633–642, and I. A. Imobighe, "An African High Command: The Search for a Feasible Strategy of Continental Defense," *African Affairs* 79 (April 1980), pp. 24–54.

31. Cynthia H. Enloe, *Ethnic Soldiers: State Security in Divided Societies* (Athens: University of Georgia Press, 1980), p. 3.

32. Ross K. Baker, "Tropical Africa's Nascent Navies," *U.S. Naval Institute Proceedings* 95, no. 1 (Januray 1969), pp. 64–71; Richard W. Hale, "The Fledgling Navies of Black Africa," *Naval War College Review* 24, no. 2 (June 1977), pp. 42–55; "Starting a Navy From Scratch: The First Twenty Years of the Congolese

23. Perkins, "Winning Friends," p. 41.

24. U.S. Congress, House of Representatives, Committee on Foreign Affairs, *Changing Perspectives on U.S. Arms Transfer Policy* (Washington, D.C.: U.S. Government Printing Office, 1981), p. 45.

25. Avery and Picard, "Pull Factors." Also see M.J.V. Bell, *Military Assistance to Independent African States*, Adelphi Papers no. 15 (London: International Institute for Strategic Studies, 1964), and Ilan Peleg, "Arms Supply to the Third World: Models and Explanations," *Journal of Modern African Studies* 15, no. 1 (March 1977), pp. 91–103.

26. Feraidoon Sham B., "American Policy: Arms and Aid in Africa," *Current History* 77, no. 488 (July/August 1979), pp. 9–13.

27. Quoted in Gregory Jaynes, "A Farewell to Africa," *New York Times Magazine*, June 28, 1981, pp. 23–40.

28. See Raymond W. Copson, "African International Politics: Underdevelopment and Conflict in the Seventies," *Orbis* 22, no. 1 (Spring 1978), pp. 227–245, and Colin Legum, I. William Zartman, Steven Langdon, and Lynn K. Mytelka, *Africa in the 1980s* (New York: McGraw-Hill, 1979).

29. See Ernest W. Lefever, *Spear and Scepter: Army, Police, and Politics in Tropical Africa* (Washington, D.C.: Brookings Institution, 1970).

30. Quoted in Stockholm International Peace Research Institute, *The Arms Trade With the Third World*, rev. and abr. ed. (New York: Holmes and Meier, 1975), p. 232.

31. Peter Grose, "Third World Nations at U.N. Show Interest in Curbs on Arms Sales," *New York Times*, October 4, 1976, and Chuck Doe, "Foreign Customers Want Best Planes," *Army Times*, December 27, 1982, pp. 14–15.

32. Gregory Copley, "Africa Begins the Change," *Defense and Foreign Affairs Digest* 7, no. 10 (1979), pp. 6–13.

33. "Armed Forces a Cash Priority," *Financial Times* (London), November 2, 1981, p. 2, sec. 2.

34. Quoted in Defense Marketing Service, *Intelligence Newsletter*, September 22, 1980, p. 3.

35. "U.S. Arms Accord with Somalia Alarms Rival Neighbor Kenya," *Washington Post*, October 20, 1980.

36. "Somalia Peeved About 'Slow' Pace of U.S. Military Aid," *Christian Science Monitor*, December 7, 1981; "Sudan Calls U.S. Aid Deficient," *New York Times*, October 20, 1981; and Alan Cowell, "Somalia's Deep Trouble as a Client State," *New York Times*, November 1, 1981, p. E5.

37. Robert I. Rotberg, "Sudan Needs Butter More Than Guns," *Christian Science Monitor*, December 7, 1981. This was evident also in the U.S. decision to provide defensive weapons only to Somalia. The Somalis apparently sought to rearm in order to continue the war with Ethiopia in the Ogaden. See Wilson, "Panel Cool."

38. Anthony Sampson, *The Arms Bazaar* (New York: Viking, 1978). For an excellent example of this type of occurrence, see Martin Edmonds, "Civil War and Arms Sales: The Nigerian-Biafran War and Other Cases," in R.D.S. Higham, ed., *Civil Wars of the Twentieth Century* (Lexington: University of Kentucky Press, 1972), pp. 203–216.

39. Testimony of Ross K. Baker in U.S. Congress, House of Representatives, Committee on Foreign Affairs, *Military Assistance Training* (Washington, D.C.: U.S. Government Printing Office, 1970), p. 114.

40. See Harkavy, *The Arms Trade and International Systems*; Edward A. Kolodziej, "Measuring French Arms Transfers: A Problem of Sources and Sources of Problems," *Journal of Conflict Resolution* 23, no. 2 (June 1979), pp. 195–227; and Edward T. Fei, "Understanding Arms Transfers and Military Expenditures: Data Problems," in Stephanie Neuman and Robert Harkavy, eds., *Arms Transfers in the Modern World* (New York: Praeger, 1979), pp. 37–46.

41. Edward J. Laurance and Ronald G. Sherwin, "Understanding Arms Transfers Through Data Analysis," pp. 87–106, and Amelia C. Leiss, "International Transfers of Armaments: Can Social Scientists Deal with Qualitative Issues?" pp. 107–117, in Uri Ra'anan, Robert L. Pfaltzgraff, Jr., and Geoffrey Kemp, eds., *Arms Transfers to the Third World: The Military Buildup in Less Industrial Countries* (Boulder, CO: Westview Press, 1978).

42. See Neuman and Harkavy, *Arms Transfers in the Modern World*, and refer to USACDA, *World Military Expenditures and Arms Transfers*, for various years. The most important consideration with such studies is to insure that the data are properly disaggregated. For example, one of the current controversies in the arms-transfer analytical community focuses on whether the United States or the USSR is the leading supplier of arms to the Third World. Aggregate data would seem to indicate U.S. leadership in the area, but when the data are further broken down, this rather misleading interpretation is dispelled. See "What Does a Soldier Cost?" *South*, July 1982, pp. 8–9, for a particularly clear case of such an interpretation. For a rejoinder, see U.S. Department of State, *Conventional Arms Transfers in the Third World, 1972–1981*, Special Report no. 102 (Washington, D.C.: U.S. Government Printing Office, 1982).

43. See S. P. Gilbert, "Soviet-American Military Aid Competition in the Third World," *Orbis* 13, no. 4 (Winter 1970), pp. 1117–1137; Lawrence Baraebibai Ekpebu, "An African Perspective on US/USSR/China Arms Policies," *Alternatives* 6, no. 1 (March 1980), pp. 93–129; and Marina S. Ottaway, *Soviet and American Influence in the Horn of Africa* (New York: Praeger, 1982).

44. Alvin Z. Rubinstein, *Soviet Foreign Policy Since World War II: Imperial and Global* (Cambridge, MA: Winthrop Publishing, 1980).

45. Edward Giraudet, "Discord in the Horn of Africa as U.S., Soviets Come Courting," *Christian Science Monitor*, January 19, 1982, p. 14.

46. Anatoly Gromyko, "Soviet Foreign Policy and Africa," *Journal of International Affairs*, reprinted in *Soviet Press: Selected Translations*, no. 82*6 (June 1982), pp. 202–207.

47. See Joshua Wynfred and Stephen P. Gilbert, *Arms for the Third World: Soviet Military Aid Diplomacy* (Baltimore: Johns Hopkins University Press, 1969); Colin Legum, "The U.S.S.R. and Africa: The African Environment," *Problems of Communism*, January–February 1978, pp. 1–19; and Henry Bienen, "Perspectives on Soviet Intervention in Africa," *Political Science Quarterly* 95, no. 1 (Spring 1980), pp. 31–42. Two good examples of this phenomenon are in Zambia and Botswana. Both countries feel threatened by South Africa and the possibility

of a spillover of violence from that country. The United States constrained its response to their requests for military aid because it might further destabilize the region. As a result, they have turned to the Soviets, who have provided MIG21s to Zambia and small arms and armored personnel carriers to Botswana. See U.S. Congress, Senate, Committee on Foreign Relations, *Economic Development Versus Military Expenditures in Countries Receiving U.S. Aid: Priorities and the Competition for Resources* (Washington, D.C.: U.S. Government Printing Office, 1980), and Foreign Broadcast Information Service, *Subsaharan Africa*, September 23, 1981, p. U3.

48. Center for Defense Information, "Soviet Weapons Exports: Russian Roulette in the Third World," *Defense Monitor* 3, no. 1 (January 1979), pp. 1–7.

49. "Soviet Third World Arms Sales Increased, CIA Reports," *Washington Post*, December 11, 1980, p. 27.

50. USACDA, *World Military Expenditures and Arms Transfers, 1970–1979*, p. 27.

51. Jonathan Alford, "The New Military Instruments," in E. J. Feuchtwanger and Peter Nailor, eds., *The Soviet Union and the Third World* (New York: St. Martin's Press, 1981), pp. 12–29. See also "A Soviet-Libya Swap," *Newsweek*, July 18, 1983, p. 36.

52. Movements such as the Union for the Total Independence of Angola (UNITA) in Angola and the Popular Front for the Libertion of Saguia el Hamra and Rio de Oro (Polisario) in western Sahara are especially well equipped with tanks, trucks, and surface-to-air missiles. See Richard Harwood, "Guerrillas Demonstrate High Morale," *Washington Post*, July 22, 1981, and Edward Cody, "Morocco Seeks U.S. Aid in Sahara," *Washington Post*, November 5, 1981. Of course, the ability to receive such equipment very often depends on the acquiescence or impotence of a neighboring country that permits its being used as a sanctuary by the revolutionary force, or its control of sizable portions of its own national territory.

53. Gavriel D. Ra'anan, *The Evolution of the Soviet Use of Surrogates in Military Relations with the Third World, with Particular Emphasis on Cuban Participation in Africa* (Santa Monica, CA.: RAND Corporation, 1979), Paper no. P-6420, p. 33.

54. Gerald T. Bender, quoted in Center for Defense Information, "Soviet Weapons Exports," p. 13.

55. "Angola Tilts Westward," *Newsweek*, May 3, 1982, p. 9.

56. Pierre, *Global Politics of Arms Sales*, pp. 73–78.

57. Leo Tansky, "Soviet Military Aid, Technical Assistance, and Academic Training," in Raymond W. Duncan, ed., *Soviet Policy in Developing Countries* (London: Cass, 1979), p. 45. Also see Central Intelligence Agency (CIA), National Foreign Assessment Center, "Communist Aid Activities in Non-Communist Less Developed Countries, 1979 and 1954–79," Report no. ER 80-10318U (October 1980), and U.S. Department of State, *Soviet and East European Aid to the Third World, 1981* (Washington, D.C.: U.S. Government Printing Office, 1983), pp. 12–15.

58. Anthony H. Cordesman, "Lessons of the Iran-Iraq War, Part Two: Tactics, Technology, and Training," *Armed Forces Journal International* (June 1982), pp. 68–85.

59. John M. Ostheimer and Gary J. Buckley, "Nigeria," in E. Kolodziej and R. Harkavy, eds., *Security Policies of Developing Countries* (Lexington, MA: D. C. Heath, 1982), pp. 285–303.

60. Jay Ross, "Ethiopia Leans Uneasily on Soviets as Reliable Source of Arms," *Washington Post*, December 31, 1981.

61. See USACDA, *World Military Expenditures and Arms Transfers, 1970–1979*, p. 27, and Jonathan Alford, "The New Military Instruments," p. 19. In the first study, comparing amounts spent on weapons systems, spares, and training, the ratio for the United States is 35:35:30, whereas for the Soviets, 70 to 80 percent is devoted to weapons and 20 to 30 percent to spares and training. In the second study, comparing weapons, support, and infrastructure, the U.S. ratio is 35:35:30 and the USSR ratio is 60:33:7. Much of this discrepancy may be attributed to the United States (and its allies generally) adopting what is known as a "total systems approach," which includes (and in fact requires) that an arms transfer include sufficient training and spares to support a weapons system during the initial period of acquisition. The Soviets seem to have adopted a radically different approach, in which they provide equipment without a support package. Perhaps the most glaring examples of this were in Egypt, where AK-47 rifles were provided without spares or maintenance literature, artillery shells came without fuses, and Soviet advisors refused to train Egyptian technicians to operate the SAM (Surface to Air Missiles) system.

62. David Lamb, "East Bloc Aid Little Comfort to Angola," *Los Angeles Times*, May 21, 1980, and Michael Goldsmith, "Madagascar Receives Arms from Soviets, Claims Nonalignment," *Los Angeles Times*, October 25, 1981.

63. John M. Starrels, *East Germany: Marxist Mission in Africa* (Washington, D.C.: Heritage Foundation, 1981); John Burns, "East German Afrika Corps," *New York Times*, November 18, 1979; and Lt. Col. I. E. Mirghani, "Lessons from the Ogaden War," *British Army Review*, August 1981, pp. 28–33.

64. See U.S. Congress, *Military Assistance Training*, p. 119. The Soviets promised Ghana in 1966–1967 to train jet pilots in six months, something "it was manifestly impossible to do," and failed.

65. Quoted in Center for Defense Information, "Soviet Weapons Exports," p. 13.

66. Umba di Lutete, "A Zairian Perspective," in Michael Samuels, ed., *Africa and the West* (Boulder, CO: Westview Press, 1980), pp. 71–85; "Angolans Begin to Ask Just What Cuban Soldiers Are Doing for Them," *Christian Science Monitor*, December 29, 1981; Cord Meyer, "Cubans Face Humiliating Angolan Exit," *Baltimore Evening Sun*, March 5, 1982. Estimates of up to $20 million per month have been made for the cost to Angola of maintaining Cuban troops there.

67. Richard Tismar, "Angola Has Second Thoughts About Help It Gets From East Bloc," *Christian Science Monitor*, February 2, 1982, p. 6. For other examples see "Portugal/Guinea-Bissau: Defense Talks," *Defense and Foreign Affairs* (April 1982), p. i; "Mozambique: Military Accord With Portugal," *Defense and Foreign*

Affairs (May 1982), p. 27; and the discussion of Cape Verde in "Military Cooperation," *Africa*, no. 119 (July 1981), p. 14.

68. Tom Gilroy, "Red Star Dims in Africa," *Christian Science Monitor*, May 27, 1981.

69. David Binder, "Soviet Cuts Arms Aid in Favor of Economic Pledges," *New York Times*, October 21, 1979, p. 24.

70. Edwin W. Besch and Donald E. Fischer, "Soviet Weaponry: Simple, Rugged, and Reliable," *Army*, February 1982, pp. 18–24, and Tome Gilroy, "Nigeria's Love-Hate Relationship with the U.S. Blooms," *Christian Science Monitor*, October 21, 1981.

71. John F. Copper and Daniel S. Papp, eds., *Communist Nations' Military Assistance* (Boulder, CO: Westview Press, 1983).

72. Joseph P. Smaldone, "Soviet and Chinese Military Aid and Arms Transfers to Africa: A Contextual Analysis," in Warren Weinstein and Thomas H. Henrikson, eds., *Soviet and Chinese Aid to African Nations* (New York: Praeger, 1980), pp. 76–116.

73. "Chinese Air Support for Zimbabwe," *Newsweek*, February 7, 1983, p. 6. See also "PRC: Military Aid to Zaire," *Defense and Foreign Affairs* (June 1982), p. i.

74. Jay Ross, "N. Korean Advisers Arrive to Train Force in Zimbabwe," *Washington Post*, August 11, 1981; "Zimbabwe: DPRK Trained Unit Shift?" *Defense and Foreign Affairs* (April 1982), p. i; and "Zimbabwe: Follies of the Fifth Brigade," *Economist*, October 30, 1982, pp. 48–49.

75. "Bury Your Dead and Run," *Newsweek*, February 21, 1983, p. 48.

76. M. Ligot, "La Cooperation Militaire dans les Accords Passes entre la France et les Etats Africaines et Malgache d'Expression Francaise," *Revue Juridique et Politique d'Outre-Mer* 17, no. 4 (October–December 1963), pp. 517–572; Chester A. Crocker, "France's Changing Military Interests," *Africa Report* 13, no. 6 (June 1966), pp. 16–41; Moshe Ammi-Oz, "Les Imperatifs de la Politique Militaire Francaise en Afrique Noire a l'Epoque de la Decolonisation," *Revue Francaise d'Etudes Politiques Africaines*, no. 134 (February 1977), pp. 65–89; and I. William Zartman, "Les Transferts d'Armements en Afrique," *Etudes Internationales* 8, no. 3 (September 1977), pp. 478–486.

77. Pierre Lellouche and Dominique Moisi, "French Policy in Africa: A Lonely Battle Against Destabilization," *International Security* 3, no. 4 (Spring 1979), pp. 108–133.

78. Senghor, "Africa and America," p. 19; Samuel F. Wells, Jr., "The Mitterrand Challenge," *Foreign Policy*, no. 44 (Fall 1981), pp. 57–69; and "French African Economies: The Empire Stays Put," *Economist*, July 10, 1982, pp. 66–67.

79. "France Speeds Up the Arms Race in Africa," *South*, May 1982, pp. 19–21.

80. Daniel Volman, "Gendarme of Africa," *The Progressive* (March 1981); Jack Kramer, "Our French Connection in Africa," *Foreign Policy*, no. 29 (Winter 1977–78), pp. 160–166; James O. Goldsborough, "Dateline Paris: Africa's Policeman," *Foreign Policy*, no. 33 (Winter 1978–79), pp. 174–190; and Walter Schutze, "The French Commitment in Africa," *Military Technology* 3, no. 7 (January–February 1979), pp. 104–112.

81. Richard Eder, "Mitterrand Tells the Africans France Will Keep Up Its Aid," *New York Times*, November 4, 1981, p. A15.

82. "France: Nous Aussi, Nous Avons Nos Falklands," *Economist*, January 22, 1983, pp. 40–41; "France and Africa: La Meme Chose," *Economist*, May 29, 1982, pp. 52–53; Col. Andre L. Rilhac, "Armor in French Rapid Assistance Forces," *Armor* 41, no. 4 (September–October 1982), pp. 20–22; June Kronholz, "France's Role in Africa: The Colonial Master Who Didn't Go Home," *Wall Street Journal*, July 22, 1981, p. 1; and Felix Kessler, "Zaire's Ills, Changed French Attitudes Signal Challenges to U.S. Africa Goals," *Wall Street Journal*, September 14, 1981, p. 34.

83. Lamiri Chirouf, "The French Debate: Arms Sales," *Adieu Report* (July–August 1981), pp. 15–17; "Mitterrand Writes a Cheque for Foreign Arms Makers," *Economist*, May 23, 1981, pp. 67–68; and "Will Mitterrand Really Crack Down on Weapons Exports?" *World Business Weekly*, July 20, 1981, pp. 22–23.

84. See *DMS International Defense Intelligence*, September 1, 1980, and October 13, 1980. In the former, General A. M. Salaam, Somali defense minister, is quoted as saying, "France is ready to sell us weapons, but we have to find the money for them because their attitude is strictly commercial." The latter newsletter reported French offers to sell arms to Sudan on credit. Although French arms are generally considered more sophisticated than Soviet, the after-sale support is looked upon as inferior to that rendered by the Americans. See "Greece: The Sale of the Decade," *Economist*, February 19, 1983, pp. 43–44.

85. Jefferey J. Carnel, "France: No. 3 Arms Merchant to the World," *Christian Science Monitor*, January 27, 1981, p. 3. An excellent example of this discretion on the part of the French is their secretly rushing arms to Cameroon during its recent border conflict with Nigeria. See "France and Africa: La Meme Chose."

86. Ulrich Albrecht and Birgit A. Sommer, *Deutsche Waffen fur die Dritte Welt: Militar hilfe und Entwicklungs politik* (Reinbeck bei Hamburg: Rowolt Taschenbuch Verlag, 1972); Jurgen Ostrowsky, "Militarische Kooperation Bundesrepublik-Sudafrika: Zu einem Memorandum des Auswartigem Amtes," *Blatter fur Deutsche und Internationale Politik* 22, no. 5 (May 1977), pp. 574–592; "West Germany: Who Wants to Sell Arms?" *Economist*, January 13, 1979, pp. 42–43; Bradley Graham, "West Germany Probes Arms Shipments to Trouble Spots," *Washington Post*, August 9, 1980, p. 20; "West Germany Debates Role of Arms Industry," *New York Times*, August 11, 1980, p. D1; and Udo Phipp, "German Arms Exports: The Debate Warms Up," *International Defense Review* 14, no. 4 (April 1981), pp. 417–420.

87. Quoted in Gary Yerkey, "European Armsmakers Aim for the Third World," *Christian Science Monitor*, March 12, 1981, p. 1.

88. Pierre, *The Global Politics of Arms Sales*, p. 109.

89. Lawrence Freedman, "Britain and the Arms Trade," *International Affairs* 54, no. 1 (July 1978), pp. 377–392; Martin Edmonds, "The Domestic and International Dimensions of British Arms Sales, 1966–1978," in Cannizzo, ed., *The Gun Merchants*, pp. 68–100. The *DMS International Defense Intelligence*, December 3, 1979, reported that British arms sales doubled between 1973 and 1978.

90. "Want a Navy Cheap? British Cuts Could Mean Big Sales," *Baltimore Sun,* August 4, 1981, p. 4, and Max Hastings and Simon Jenkins, *The Battle for the Falklands* (New York: Norton, 1983).

91. See "British Help for Ugandan Army Welcomed," *Christian Science Monitor,* July 20, 1981, and "British General Sizing Up Zimbabwe on Need for Aid," *Christian Science Monitor,* July 24, 1981.

92. Michael J. Christie, *The Simonstown Agreement: Britain's Defence and the Sale of Arms to South Africa* (London: Africa Bureau, 1970); and Isebill V. Gruhn, "British Arms Sales to South Africa: The Limits of African Diplomacy," *Studies in Race and Nations* 3, no. 3 (Winter 1971–72), pp. 1–30.

93. L. Heinman, "Military Assistance by Small Nations," *Military Review,* no. 44 (March 1964), pp. 14–18; Bernard Udis, *From Guns to Butter: Technology, Organizations, and Reduced Military Spending in Europe* (Cambridge, MA: Ballinger, 1978); and Murray Seeger, "West European Arms Industry Seeks to Concentrate Firepower," *Los Angeles Times,* July 19, 1981, p. 1F.

94. Gary Yerkey, "Belgium Embroiled in Controversy Over Sale of Military Hardware to Foreign Governments," *Christian Science Monitor,* January 6, 1981, p. 10; and Warren Weinstein, "The Limits of Military Dependency: The Case of Belgian Military Aid to Burundi, 1961–1973," *Journal of African Studies* 2, no. 3 (Fall 1975), pp. 419–431. *DMS International Defense Intelligence,* June 16, 1980, reported that Belgian arms sales were up 25 percent in 1979–1980 despite complaints by the Socialist party concerning human rights.

95. Fabrizio Battistelli and Gianluca Devoto, "Italian Military Policy and the Arms Industry," *Lo Spettore Internazionale,* no. 9 (July–December 1974), pp. 197–221.

96. "Arms Exporter Faces Challenge in Neutral Austria," *New York Times,* March 15, 1981, p. 20.

97. Clyde Sanger, "Canada and Africa: Aid and Politics," *Africa Report* 15, no. 4 (April 1970), pp. 12–15; William Cobban, "Dealing Out Death Discreetly: The Traffic in Canadian Arms," *Saturday Night,* no. 86 (November 1971), pp. 23–26; Douglas C. Anglin, *The International Arms Traffic in Sub-Saharan Africa,* Occasional Paper no. 12 (Ottawa: Norman Patterson School, 1971); and Ernie Regehr, *Making a Killing: Canada's Arms Industry* (Toronto: McClelland and Stewart, 1975).

98. Office of the White House Press Secretary, May 19, 1977, "Statement by the President on Conventional Arms Transfer Policy."

99. U.S. Congress, Senate, Committee on Foreign Relations, *Implications of President Carter's Conventional Arms Transfer Policy* (Washington, D.C.: U.S. Government Printing Office, 1977); Sen. Dick Clark and Bernard A. Schriever, "U.S. Arms Sales Abroad: A Policy of Restraint?" *AEI Defense Review* 2, no. 5 (1978), entire issue; *DMS International Defense Intelligence,* October 31, 1979, listed a number of arms sales lost to the British and French because of Carter administration denials.

100. Office of the White House Press Secretary, "Text of President Ronald Reagan's July 8, 1981, Arms Transfer Policy Directive"; Judith Miller, "Buckley, Outlining Reagan Policy, Calls Arms Sales a 'Vital' Tool," *New York Times,* May

22, 1981, p. A12; "Arms Sales Defended by U.S. Official," *Washington Star*, July 29, 1981, p. 6; and Roger P. Labrie, John G. Hutchins, and Edwin W. A. Peura, *U.S. Arms Sales Policy: Background and Issues* (Washington, D.C.: American Enterprise Institute, 1982).

101. Senator Proxmire is quoted in "U.S. Weapons Exports Headed For Record Level," *Defense Monitor* 11, no. 3 (March 1982), p. 5. Examples of criticism on the policy are found in Barry M. Blechman, Janne E. Nolan, and Alan Platt, "Pushing Arms," *Foreign Policy*, no. 46 (Spring 1982), pp. 134–154; "Arms Sales: Boom Time," *Economist*, July 4, 1981, p. 26; "Reagan's Arms Sales Drive," *Newsweek*, August 3, 1981, p. 26; and Walter S. Mossberg, "Administration Split Over Who Gets F16 First," *Wall Street Journal*, June 23, 1981, p. 35.

102. William P. Clark, "National Security Strategy" (speech presented at the Georgetown University Center for Strategic and International Studies, Washington, D.C., May 21, 1982). See also Chester A. Crocker, *Challenge to Regional Security in Africa*, Current Policy no. 431 (Washington, D.C.: Department of State, 1982); and James L. Buckley, *Security Assistance for FY 1983*, Current Policy no. 378 (Washington, D.C.: Department of State, 1982).

103. Quoted in Richard Halloran, "Special U.S. Force for Persian Gulf is Growing Swiftly," *New York Times*, October 25, 1982, p. A1. See also "Rapid Deployment Force: Will Europe Help America Help Europe?" *Economist*, December 11, 1982, p. 62.

104. Benjamin F. Schemmer, "The U.S. Has Lost a Lot of Years" (interview with Lt. Gen. Mahamed Abu-Ghazala, Egyptian defense minister), *Armed Forces Journal International*, September 1981, pp. 46–51, and Henry S. Bradsher, "U.S., Kenya in Accord on Allowing Greater Use of Port Facilities," *Washington Star*, June 28, 1980.

105. Henry Bienen, "U.S. Foreign Policy in a Changing Africa," *Political Science Quarterly* 93, no. 3 (Fall 1978), pp. 443–464; Gary Wasserman, "The Foreign Aid Dilemma," *Washington Quarterly* 6, no. 1 (Winter 1983), pp. 96–106; and David Douglas, "Calling Aid by Its Right Name," *Christian Science Monitor*, November 25, 1981.

106. John de St. Jorre, "Africa: Crisis of Confidence," *Foreign Affairs* 61, no. 3 (America and the World, 1982), pp. 675–691.

107. Quoted in Alan Cowell, "In Sudan, 220 Miles Can Last Forever," *New York Times*, November 2, 1981, p. A3. Also see Helen Kitchen, "Six Misconceptions of Africa," *Washington Quarterly* 5, no. 4 (Autumn 1982), pp. 167–174.

108. Judith Miller, "Third World Lands Join Ranks of Arms Exporters," *New York Times*, December 13, 1981. See the introduction to Kolodziej and Harkavy, eds., *Security Policies of Developing Countries*. See also *Latin America Weekly Report* (June 20, 1980), p. 4.

109. Michael T. Kaufman, "22 Countries Avail Themselves of Pakistani Soldiers," *New York Times*, February 6, 1981, p. A2, and William Drozdiak, "Egypt Supplying Arms to Rebels Fighting in Chad," *Washington Star*, March 17, 1981, p. 1. The issue of retransfers of arms is a serious one. A colleague of mine reports that automatic weapons making their way from Uganda to northern Kenya are being used by pastoral peoples against their traditional

enemies with devastating effect—entire bands or villages are being wiped out, and the refugee problem exacerbated as the survivors flee.

110. Everett G. Martin, "Latin Leader: Brazil Increases Exports of Technology with Governments, Setting Pace in Third World," *Wall Street Journal*, October 6, 1981.

111. Daniela Pinto, "Brazil's Africa Connections," *Africa*, no. 113 (June 1981), pp. 11–15; "Brazil: A Major Contender in the Arms Business," *Business Week*, July 31, 1978, pp. 45–46; Warren Hoge, "Brazil's Arms Find Willing Buyers in the Third World," *New York Times*, August 9, 1981, p. E3; Jim Brooke, "Brazil Rapidly Becomes Global Giant in Sale of Weapons," *Miami Herald*, October 6, 1981; and "Gabon to Receive Brazilian Armoured Vehicles," *Defence Africa*, September–October 1981, p. 28.

112. Jim Brooke, "Dateline Brazil: Southern Superpower," *Foreign Policy*, no. 44 (Fall 1981), pp. 167–180; William Perry, "Military Policy and Conventional Capabilities of an Emerging Power," *Military Review*, September 1978, pp. 10–24; and Frank D. McCann, Jr., "The Brazilian Army and the Pursuit of Arms Independence, 1899–1979," in B. F. Cooling, ed., *War, Business, and the World Military-Industrial Complex* (London: Kennikat Press, 1981), pp. 171–193.

113. Paul L. Moorcraft, "The MIC Under Siege: The White Redoubt in Africa," in Cooling, ed., *War, Business, and the World Military-Industrial Complex*, pp. 194–208; Geoffrey Kemp, "South Africa's Defence Programme," *Survival* 14, no. 4 (July–August 1972), pp. 158–161; Chester A. Crocker, "Current and Projected Military Balances in Southern Africa," in Richard Bissell and Chester Crocker, eds., *South Africa Into the 1980s* (Boulder, CO: Westview Press, 1979), pp. 71–106; Bernard Simon, "Pretoria Aims for Sales to Foreign Arsenals," *Financial Times* (London), September 14, 1982; "Mozambique: Hands (and Arms) Across the Border," *Economist*, June 12, 1982; and "There's a New Armored War Being Fought," *Defense and Foreign Affairs* (January/February 1982), pp. 6–8.

114. Abel Jacob, "Israel's Military Aid to Africa, 1960–1966," *Journal of Modern African Studies* 9, no. 2 (August 1971), pp. 165–187; Drew Middleton, "South Africa Needs More Arms, Israeli Says," *New York Times*, December 14, 1981, p. A9; and "Arms Are a Crucial Export for Israel," *New York Times*, August 24, 1981, p. A3.

115. George Lardner, Jr., "Mobutu Says Zaire Is Ready to Renew Its Ties With Israel," *Washington Post*, December 3, 1981, and "Israelis Will Reshape Zaire's Armed Forces," *New York Times*, January 20, 1983.

116. See Ostheimer and Buckley, "Nigeria."

117. Baldes Raj Nayar, "Political Mainsprings of Economic Planning in the New Nations," *Comparative Politics* 6, no. 3 (Fall 1974), pp. 341–366, and Michael Moodie, "Sovereignty, Security, and Arms," *Washington Papers* 8, no. 67 (1979), pp. 11–15.

118. Agrippah T. Mugomba, *The Foreign Policy of Despair: Africa and the Sale of Arms to South Africa* (Nairobi: East Africa Literature Bureau, 1977); Caryle Murphy, "Embargo Spurs S. Africa to Build Weapons Industry," *Washington Post*, July 7, 1981; and "Pretoria Produces Most of Its Weapons at Home," *Chicago Sun*, February 28, 1982.

Chapter 4

1. *New conventional weapons* are usually considered to include precision, terminally guided munitions and their delivery systems. See Jacquelyn K. Davis, Robert W. Helm, and G. Phillip Hughes, "An Inventory of New Weapons Systems for Non-Nuclear Combat," in Geoffrey A. Kemp, Robert L. Pfaltzgraff, Jr., and Uri Ra'anan, eds., *The Other Arms Race: New Technologies and Non-Nuclear Conflict* (Lexington, MA: D. C. Heath, 1975), p. 156, and Christoph Bertram, ed., *New Conventional Weapons and East-West Security* (New York: Praeger, 1978).

2. See "How Pave Movers and Wasps Will Help to Hold the NATO Line," *Economist*, December 11, 1982, pp. 41–42.

3. Hugh Sidey, "We're Captives of War Technology," *Chicago Sun-Times*, August 23, 1981, p. 7E.

4. See Warren F. Ilchman and Norman Thomas Uphoff, *The Political Economy of Change* (Berkeley: University of California Press, 1969).

5. For a review of these arguments, see Fredrick S. Paerson, "U.S. Arms Transfers: The Feasibility of Restraint," *Arms Control* 2 (May 1981), pp. 25–49.

6. Ali A. Mazrui, *Africa's International Relations: The Diplomacy of Dependency and Change* (Boulder, CO: Westview Press, 1977).

7. David Moore, "United States Aid and the Arms Trade," *Current History* 77, no. 448 (July–August 1979), pp. 5–8, 34–35.

8. See Chapter 2.

9. For a recent example, see Avi Plascov, *Security in the Persian Gulf: Modernization, Political Development, and Stability* (London: International Institute for Strategic Studies, 1982), pp. 100–109.

10. See Francis M. Deng, "Security Problems: An African Predicament," and D. Katete Orwa, "National Security An African Perspective," in Bruce E. Arlinghaus, ed., *African Security Issues: Sovereignty, Stability, and Solidarity* (Boulder, CO: Westview Press, 1984).

11. Theodore H. Moran, "Iranian Defense Expenditures and the Social Crisis," *International Security* 3, no. 3 (Winter 1978–79), pp. 178–192.

12. Michael Moodie, "Sovereignty, Security, and Arms," *Washington Papers* 7, no. 67 (1979), p. 24.

13. Julius K. Nyerere, *Freedom and Development: A Selection From Writings and Speeches 1968–1973* (Dar es Salaam: Oxford University Press, 1973), pp. 247–248.

14. Quoted in Bernard Gwertzman, "Pakistan Balking at Jet Purchase," *New York Times*, November 30, 1982, p. A1.

15. Robert I. Rotberg, "Sudan Needs Butter More Than Guns," *Christian Science Monitor*, December 7, 1981.

16. Douglas Watson, "Poverty of Sudan Highlighted by Lack of Roads for U.S. Tanks," *Chicago Sun*, January 26, 1982. Also see Louise Lief, "Sudan Goes West," *Los Angeles Times*, October 18, 1981.

17. "I Am Still a Caretaker," *Time* (December 13, 1982), p. 46 (interview with General Zia). The importance of this perception on the part of arms

purchasers should not be underestimated. In the Pakistan case, they were offered F5G (now designated F20) fighters that were built for export and were considerably cheaper than F16s. But the Pakistanis had "vow[ed] they would never accept anything less than the best." See "Buying Insecurity," *Economist*, September 28, 1981, pp. 15–16.

18. For an appreciation of these costs see the figures in James W. Abellera, Roger P. Labrie, and Albert C. Pierce, "The FY1982–1986 Defense Program: Issues and Trends," *AEI Foreign Policy and Defense Review* 3, nos. 4 and 5 (1982), pp. 24–26.

19. "I Am Still a Caretaker," p. 46.

20. The World Bank, *Accelerated Development in Subsaharan Africa: An Agenda for Action* (Washington, D.C.: The International Bank for Reconstruction and Development, 1981), and "Africa's Growing Pains," *Economist*, October 10, 1981, pp. 88–90.

21. John D. Montgomery, *Technology and Civil Life: Making and Implementing Development Decisions* (Cambridge: MIT Press, 1974), pp. 160–161.

22. David K. Whynes, *The Economics of Third World Military Expenditure* (Austin: University of Texas Press, 1979), p. 16. Also see Shuja Nawaz, "Economic Impact of Defense Expenditures," *Finance and Development* 20, no. 1 (March 1983), pp. 34–35.

23. Altaf Gauhar, "The Hidden Cost of the Arms Race," *South*, July 1982, p. 7.

24. Lt. Col. David R. Holmes, "The Role of U.S. Security Assistance: Its Impact on the Recipient Nation," *Military Review* 58, no. 2 (February 1978), pp. 68–74.

25. Irving Louis Horowitz, *Beyond Empire and Revolution: Militarization and Consolidation in the Third World* (New York: Oxford University Press, 1982), p. 174.

26. Naomi Caiden and Aaron Wildavsky, *Planning and Budgeting in Poor Countries* (New Brunswick, NJ: Transaction Books, 1980), p. 84. Also see Dennis J. Murray and Paul R. Viotti, eds., *The Defense Policy of Nations: A Comparative Study* (Baltimore: Johns Hopkins University Press, 1982), and Stephanie Neuman, ed., *Defense Planning in Less-Industrialized Countries* (Lexington, MA: D. C. Heath, 1983).

27. Albert Watson, *Development Planning: Lessons of Experience* (Baltimore: Johns Hopkins University Press, 1979).

28. Peter Heller, "The Underfinancing of Recurrent Development Costs," *Finance and Development* 16, no. 1 (March 1979), pp. 38–41.

29. Fred Kaplan, "Defense Nuts and Bolts," *New York Times*, November 17, 1982, p. A35, and James Fallows, "Defense: What Are We Buying?" *Baltimore Sun*, July 19, 1981, p. K1.

30. See Philip Short, "Army Still Takes Biggest Slice of Uganda's Budget," *African Development* 6, (1972), pp. 15–16, and Foreign Broadcast Information Service, *Subsaharan Africa*, Report no. 2472, "Heavy Defense Budget," p. 9.

31. Quoted in "Defending the United States," *Newsweek*, December 20, 1982, pp. 22–23. Also see Walter S. Mossberg, "Pentagon Study Says Future Costs

of Arms in Buildup Plan Seriously Underestimated," *Wall Street Journal*, December 7, 1982, p. 3; Richard Halloran, "Why Defense Costs So Much," *New York Times*, January 11, 1981, p. 1, sec. 3; Michael D'Antonio, "Can the Pentagon Spend All That Money Effectively?" *Baltimore Sun*, July 19, 1981, p. K1; Walter S. Mossberg, "Weinberger Says Military Spending Rise Won't Spur Inflation or Disrupt Economy," *Wall Street Journal*, July 29, 1981, p. 12; and Robert DeGrasse, Jr., and David Gold, "Military Spending's Damage to the Economy," *New York Times*, December 29, 1981, p. A15.

32. James S. Coleman and Belmont Brice, Jr., "The Role of the Military in Sub-Saharan Africa," in John L. Johnson, ed., *The Role of the Military in Underdeveloped Countries* (Princeton: Princeton University Press, 1962), p. 395.

33. Horowitz, *Beyond Empire and Revolution*, p. xxiii.

34. Gary Zuk and William R. Thompson, "The Post-Coup Military Spending Question: A Pooled Cross Sectional Time Series Analysis," *American Political Science Review* 76, no. 1 (March 1982), pp. 60–74.

35. "Kenya: Coupables," *Economist*, January 22, 1983, p. 32.

36. Claude E. Welch, Jr., "Cincinnatus in Africa: The Possibility of Military Withdrawal from Politics," in Michael Lofchie, ed., *The State of Nations: Constraints on Development in Independent Africa* (Berkeley: University of California Press, 1971), pp. 215–237. Also see "The Myth of the Man on Horseback," *South*, July 1982, pp. 10–11.

37. Margaret Peil, "A Civilian Appraisal of Military Rule in Nigeria," *Armed Forces and Society* 2, no. 1 (November 1975), pp. 34–45.

38. I. J. Ebong, permanent secretary, Federal Ministry of Economic Development and Reconstruction, quoted in Akinsola Akiwowo, "Military Professionalism and the Crisis of Returning Power to Civilian Regimes of West Africa," *Armed Forces and Society* 3, no. 4 (Summer 1977), pp. 643–654.

39. "Zambia Chafes at IMF Terms," *New African*, April 1983, p. 26.

40. See K. Sogstad, "Utviklingen av Militaere Styrker og Muligheter for Rustningskontroll i Afrika," *Internasiornal Politikk*, no. 2 (1967), pp. 103–139, and Robin Luckham, "Armaments, Underdevelopment, and Demilitarisation in Africa," *Alternatives* 6, no. 2 (July 1980), pp. 179–245.

41. Helena Tuomi and Raimo Vayrynen, *Transnational Corporations, Armaments, and Development* (New York: St. Martin's, 1982), pp. 215–220.

42. Peter Lock and Herbert Wulf, "The Economic Consequences of the Transfer of Military-Oriented Technology," in Mary Kaldor and Absjorn Eide, eds., *The World Military Order: The Impact of Military Technology in the Third World* (New York: Praeger, 1980), pp. 210–231.

43. See Holmes, "The Role of U.S. Security Assistance."

44. See Bahram Nowzad, "Debt in Developing Countries: Some Issues for the 1980s," *Finance and Development* 19, no. 1 (March 1982), pp. 13–16; Millard Long and Frank Veneroso, "The Debt-Related Problems of the Non-Oil Producing Less Developed Countries," *Economic Development and Cultural Change* 29, no. 3 (April 1981), pp. 501–516; "IMF View of the African Economy," *African Business*, July 1981, pp. 15–17; "A Nightmare of Debt: A Survey of International Banking," *Economist*, March 20, 1982; "Zaire: The Squeeze Hurts," *Economist*,

October 17, 1981, p. 38; "Sudan: The Other Enemy," *Economist,* November 14, 1981, p. 38; and "Sudan Goes Bust," *Economist,* February 20, 1982, pp. 55–56, wherein a foreign banker states: "No manufacturer in his right mind is prepared to do business with Sudan on a credit basis anymore." There is good reason for this concern. Sudan has the highest debt-service payments in Africa and serious balance-of-payments problems. See Barbara Crossette, "U.S. Seems Unsure About Speeding Arms Flow to Sudan," *New York Times,* October 14, 1981.

45. See Emile Benoit, *Defense and Economic Growth in Developing Countries* (Lexington, MA: D. C. Heath, 1973), and the discussion in Chapter 1 of this book.

46. Quoted in James Reston, "The Meaning of Security," *New York Times,* May 25, 1979.

Chapter 5

1. Anthony Pascal, *Are Third World Armies Third Rate? Human Capital and Organizational Impediments to Military Effectiveness* (Santa Monica, CA: RAND Corporation, 1980), Report no. P-6433, pp. 1–8.

2. Douglas Watson, "Poverty of Sudan Highlighted by Lack of Roads for U.S. Tanks," *Chicago Sun,* January 26, 1982.

3. Robert I. Rotberg, "Sudan Needs Butter More Than Guns," *Christian Science Monitor,* December 7, 1981.

4. Theodore H. Moran, "Iranian Defense Expenditures and the Social Crisis," *International Security* 3, no. 3 (Winter 1978–79), pp. 178–192.

5. U.S. Congress, Senate, Committee on Foreign Relations, *U.S. Military Sales to Iran* (Washington, D.C.: U.S. Government Printing Office, 1976), pp. viii–xii. It is interesting to note that in the Iran-Iraq war, it is precisely those older, more absorbable F5s and F4s that are flying the majority of Iranian combat sorties; see "Turnaround on Two Fronts," *Time,* April 19, 1982, p. 19.

6. Geoffrey Kemp, "Arms Transfers and the 'Back-End' Problem in Developing Countries," in Stephanie Neuman and Robert Harkavy, eds., *Arms Transfers in the Modern World* (New York: Praeger, 1979), pp. 264–275.

7. See Geoffrey Kemp, Robert L. Pfaltzgraff, Jr., Uri Ra'anan, and Charles M. Perry, "The Military Buildup in Less Industrial States: Policy Implications," in Uri Ra'anan, Robert L. Pfaltzgraff, Jr., and Geoffrey Kemp, eds., *Arms Transfers to the Third World: The Military Buildup in Less Industrialized Countries* (Boulder, CO: Westview Press, 1978), pp. 391–411.

8. "With 40% Illiteracy, Those Who Start an Education Usually Don't Finish It," *Chicago Tribune,* February 25, 1982, p. A4.

9. Ray Moseley, "Education Not Meeting Today's Needs," *Chicago Tribune,* October 1, 1981. Also see William R. Cotter, "How AID Fails to Aid Africa," *Foreign Policy,* no. 34 (Spring 1979), pp. 107–119.

10. "Doubts Mounting About All-Volunteer Force," *Science* 209 (September 5, 1980), pp. 1095–1099.

11. Alvin J. Cottrell, Robert Hanks, and Michael Moodie, *Arms Transfers and U.S. Foreign and Military Policy*, Significant Issues ser. (Washington, D.C.: Georgetown University Center for Strategic and International Studies, 1980), pp. 39–40.

12. Michael Moodie, "Arms Transfer Policy: A National Dilemma," *Washington Quarterly* 5, no. 2 (Spring 1982), pp. 109–112.

13. "U.S., in Shift, Cuts Aid to Zaire and Assists Nigeria," *New York Times*, January 16, 1978, p. A7.

14. Thomas J. Faver, *War Clouds on the Horn of Africa; The Widening Storm*, 2d. rev. ed. (Washington, D.C.: Carnegie Endowment, 1979), p. 115, and Drew Middleton, "A Sudan War: Beyond Libya's Means," *New York Times*, October 23, 1981.

15. "Fifth Brigade to Get N. Korean Tanks," *Herald* (Salisbury/Harare), August 22, 1981, p. 1.

16. David Ignatius, "African Hot Spot: Sudan Facing a Threat From Quadaffi, Is Beset by Problems at Home," *Wall Street Journal*, October 13, 1981.

17. See two "Sixty Minutes" broadcasts, "What About the U.N.?" (November 15, 1981) and "Fakes" (December 27, 1981), for examples.

18. Pascal, *Are Third World Armies Third Rate?* p. 21.

19. National Guard Bureau, "Vista 1999: A Long-Range Look at the Future of the Army and Air National Guard" (March 1982, mimeo), p. 60.

20. Anthony H. Cordesman, "Lessons of the Iran-Iraq War, Part Two: Tactics, Technology and Training," *Armed Forces Journal International*, June 1982, pp. 68–85.

21. See Henry Bienen, "Military and Society in East Africa: Thinking Again About Praetorianism," *Comparative Politics* 6, no. 1 (Winter 1974), pp. 489–517, and Issac James Mowoe, ed., *The Performance of Soldiers as Governors: African Politics and the African Military* (Washington, D.C.: University Press of America, 1980), especially the case studies dealing with the Congo, Mali, and Zaire.

22. Col. Norman Dodd, "Kenya's Armed Forces," *Defence Africa*, November/December 1981, pp. 4–7.

23. Alan Cowell, "Ethiopian Drive Against Somalia Bogs Down," *New York Times*, October 8, 1982, p. A1. For Angolan and other examples, see discussions of Soviet arms transfers in Chapter 3.

24. Alan Cowell, "Foreigners Vital to Zaire's Forces," *New York Times*, August 16, 1981, p. 8.

25. "America's Help Called Key to Libya's Move Into Chad," *New York Times*, November 1, 1981. In addition to U.S. technicians considered "indispensable" to flying and maintaining Libyan air force equipment, British pilots were also reported flying C130 transport aircraft.

26. Jay Ross, "How Kenya's Rebels Botched Their Coup," *Washington Post*, August 9, 1982.

27. J. A. Stockfish, *Ploughshares Into Swords: Managing the American Defense Establishment* (New York: Mason and Lipscomb, 1973), p. 150.

28. Jo L. Husbands, "The Long, Long Pipeline: Arms Sales and Technological Dependence in the Third World" (CACI, Inc., Washington, D.C., 1978, mimeo).

29. James R. Carleton, "NATO Standardization: An Organizational Analysis," in L. S. Kaplan and R. W. Clawson, eds., *NATO After Thirty Years* (Wilmington, DE: Scholarly Resources, Inc., 1982), pp. 199–214, and Government Accounting Office, *Increased Standardization Would Reduce Costs of Ground Support Equipment For Military Aircraft* (Washington, D.C.: U.S. Government Printing Office, 1980), Report no. LCD-80-30. For example, the U.S. Department of Defense alone requires 129 types of tow bars, 71 kinds of boarding ladders, and 111 different aircraft engine maintenance stands. The terms *rationalization, standardization,* and *interoperability* may be unfamiliar to those outside the military. *Rationalization* refers to the overall program of defense coordination (internally or among allies), and it includes *standardization* (common equipment), *interoperability* (the ability to function together without difficulty, e.g., all measurements will be metric), and other activities such as cooperation in training and doctrine. Ultimately, these terms relate to the creation of military synergies—the making of a military capability that is greater than the sum of its component parts. See Trevor Taylor, *Defence, Technology, and International Integration* (London: Frances Pinter, 1982), p. 11.

30. "America's Newest Ally," *Newsweek*, October 26, 1981, p. 29.

31. "Sudan's Leader Predicts an Invasion by Libyans," *New York Times*, October 13, 1981, p. A1.

32. Sharam Chubin, "Implications of the Military Buildup in Less Industrial States: The Case of Iran," in Ra'anan, Pfaltzgraff, and Kemp, eds., *Arms Transfers to the Third World*, p. 257.

33. Leo Tansky, "Soviet Military Aid, Technical Assistance and Academic Training," in Raymond W. Duncan, ed., *Soviet Policy in the Third World* (London: Pergamon, 1979), p. 45. For a specific description of some of these problems in Africa, see Don Parry, "Military Electronics for Africa," *Defence Africa*, September–October 1981, pp. 9–10.

34. Art Pine, "Sub-Sahara Countries Take First Steps to End Economic Nightmare," *Wall Street Journal*, September 16, 1982, p. 1. Also see Uma Lele, "Rural Africa: Modernization, Equity, and Long-Term Development," *Science* 211 (February 6, 1981), pp. 547–553.

35. Peter Kilby, "What Oil Wealth Did to Nigeria," *Wall Street Journal*, November 25, 1981, p. 26.

36. Massiye Edwin Koloko, *The Manpower Approach to Planning: Theoretical Issues and Evidence From Zambia* (Denver: University of Denver, 1980), p. 2.

37. Government of Kenya, *Five Year Development Plan* (Nairobi: Government Publishing Office, 1978), p. 481.

38. International Labour Organization (ILO), *Employment, Incomes, and Equality: A Strategy for Increasing Productive Employment in Kenya* (Geneva: ILO, 1972); Edgar O. Edwards, ed., *Employment in Developing Nations* (New York: Columbia University Press, 1974); and Ukandi G. Damachi and Victor P. Diejomaoh, eds., *Human Resources and African Development* (New York: Praeger, 1978).

39. Koloko, *The Manpower Approach to Planning*, p. 75.

40. Ronald P. Dore, *The Diploma Disease: Education, Qualification, and Development* (Berkeley: University of California Press, 1976), and Guy Hunter,

Modernizing Peasant Societies: A Comparative Study in Asia and Africa (New York: Oxford University Press, 1969), p. 248.

41. Remi Clignet, "Educational and Occupational Differentiation in a New Country: The Case of the Cameroon," *Economic Development and Cultural Change* 25 (September 1977), pp. 731–745.

42. Gary S. Fields, "The Private Demand for Education in Relation to the Labour Market Conditions in Less Developed Countries," in D. Ghai and M. Godfrey, eds., *Essays on Employment in Kenya* (Nairobi: Kenya Literature Bureau, 1978).

43. United Nations, Economic Commission for Africa, *Economic Bulletin for Africa* 10, no. 1 (June 1970).

44. Robert D. Loken, *Manpower Development in Africa* (New York: Praeger, 1969), p. 7.

45. C. P. Thakur, "Skill Generation and Labor Market in a Developing Country," *Economic Development and Cultural Change* 27 (April 1979), pp. 343–356.

46. Kenneth J. King, "Skill Acquisition in the Informal Sector of the Economy," in David Court and Dharam P. Ghai, eds., *Education, Society, and Development: New Perspectives from Kenya* (Nairobi: Oxford University Press), pp. 291–309.

47. Eli Ginzberg and Herbert A. Smith, *Manpower Strategy for Developing Countries: Lessons From Ethiopia* (New York: Columbia University Press, 1967), p. 43.

48. June Kronholz, "For African Countries, National Airlines Are For More Than Travel," *Wall Street Journal*, August 25, 1981, p. 1. For a discussion of how the U.S. military provides skilled labor to industry, see Lester C. Thurow, "Wanted: More Skilled Workers," *New York Times*, May 3, 1981, p. 2F.

49. Moran, "Iranian Defense Expenditures," p. 189.

50. For examples, see Patrick Marnham, *Fantastic Invasion: Notes on Contemporary Africa* (New York: Harcourt Brace Jovanovich, 1978), pp. 131–132; Edward Hoagland, *African Calliope* (London: Penguin, 1980); Xan Smiley, "Misunderstanding Africa," *Atlantic Monthly*, September 1982, pp. 70–79; and David Lamb, *The Africans* (New York: Random House, 1982).

51. Gavin Kennedy, *The Military in the Third World* (New York: Scribner's, 1974), pp. 305–315. For a detailed summary of the maintenance and logistic requirements of modern weapons, see Stockholm International Peace Research Institute, *The Arms Trade with the Third World* (London: Holmes and Meier, 1971), pp. 84–85 and app. 4. More recently, James F. Dunnigan, in *How To Make War: A Comprehensive Guide to Modern Warfare* (New York: Morrow, 1982), provides an insight into the frailty of new conventional weapons. His maxim that "as things become more expensive, they become less reliable" (p.349), effectively summarizes the situation.

52. Steven J. Rosen, "The Proliferation of New Land-Based Technologies: Implications for Local Military Balances," in Neuman and Harkavy, *Arms Transfers in the Modern World*, pp. 109–130, and Anthony Pascal et al., "Men and Arms in the Middle East: The Human Factor in Military Modernization," in Douglas J. Murray and Paul R. Viotti, eds., *The Defense Policies of Nations: A Comparative Study* (Baltimore: Johns Hopkins University Press, 1982), pp. 406–415.

53. On Zaire, see Gary Yerkey, "Troubled Zaire Finds Fewer Active Backers in the West," *Christian Science Monitor*, September 1, 1981, p. 6; Russell Warren Howe, "Mobutu Prospers, Zaire Impoverished," *Washington Times*, June 25, 1982; and U.S. Congress, House of Representatives, Committee on Foreign Affairs, *Political and Economic Situation in Zaire—Fall 1981* (Washington, D.C.: U.S. Government Printing Office, 1981). On Libya, see "Kaddafi's Dangerous Game," *Newsweek*, July 20, 1981, pp. 40–46; "Ex-Colony of Djibouti Still Relying on Former French Masters For Help," *Chicago Sun*, October 4, 1981; and "Libya: Who Laughs Last?" *Economist*, October 10, 1981, p. 53. Kenya was experiencing some difficulty with its new helicopter program: see "Copter Crash Kills Two Army Officers," *Daily Nation* (Nairobi), July 18, 1981.

54. James S. Slotkin, *From Field to Factory: New Industrial Employees* (Glencoe, IL: Glencoe Free Press, 1960).

55. Peter Kilby, "Farm and Factory: A Comparison of the Skill Requirements for the Transfer of Technology," *Journal of Development Issues* 9 (1972), pp. 63–69, and D. Babatunde Thomas, *Importing Technology Into Africa: Foreign Investment and the Supply of Technological Innovations* (New York: Praeger, 1976).

56. Solon T. Kimball and Jacquetta Burnett, eds., *Learning and Culture* (Seattle: University of Washington Press, 1973); Judith Friedman Hansen, *Sociocultural Perspectives on Human Learning: An Introduction to Educational Anthropology* (Englewood Cliffs, NJ: Prentice-Hall, 1979); Mallory Wober, *Psychology in Africa* (London: International African Institute, 1975); R. Ogbonna and Barnabas Otaala, eds., *The African Child and His Environment* (New York: Pergamon, 1981); and UNESCO, *Youth, Tradition and Development in Africa* (New York: United Nations, 1981).

57. Ulric Neisser, *Cognition and Reality: Principles and Implications of Cognitive Psychology* (San Francisco: Freeman, 1976), pp. 66–67; John W. Berry, *Human Ecology and Cognitive Style: Comparative Studies in Cultural and Psychological Adaptation* (New York: Sage, 1976), p. 31; and John W. Berry and P. R. Dasen, eds., *Culture and Cognition: Readings in Cross-Cultural Psychology* (London: Methuen, 1974).

58. T. M. Yesufu, *Manpower Problems and Economic Development in Africa* (Ibadan: Oxford University Press, 1969).

59. Robert Solo, "The Capacity to Assimilate an Advanced Technology," *American Economic Review* 56, no. 2 (1966), pp. 91–97.

60. Robert W. July, *Precolonial Africa: An Economic and Social History* (New York: Scribner's, 1975) p. 285.

61. Loken, *Manpower Development in Africa*, p. 97.

62. Cited in Robert F. Murphey, *An Overture to Social Anthropology* (Englewood Cliffs, NJ: Prentice-Hall, 1979), p. 17.

63. Richard Critchfield, "Science and the Villager: The Last Sleeper Wakes," *Foreign Affairs* 61, no. 1 (Fall 1982), pp. 14–41.

64. Sylvia Scribner and Michael Cole, *The Psychology of Literacy* (Cambridge: Harvard University Press, 1981); Carol R. Ember, "Cross-Cultural Cognitive Studies," *Annual Review of Anthropology* 6 (1977), pp. 33–56; and John Simmons, "Retention of Cognitive Skills Acquired in Primary School," *Comparative Education Review* 20 (February 1976), pp. 79–93.

65. George M. Foster, *Traditional Societies and Technological Change*, 2d. ed. (New York: Harper and Row, 1973), p. 146.

66. Government Accounting Office, *AID Must Consider Social Factors in Establishing Cooperatives in Developing Countries* (Washington, D.C.: U.S. Government Printing Office, 1980), Report no. ID-80-39.

67. See "Weapons Usage Limited by Argentine Experience," *Aviation Week and Space Technology*, May 1, 1982, p. 26. The Soviets have experienced serious problems trying to incorporate ethnic minorities into their armed forces, and there is a dramatically lower ability of Central Asian soldiers to use technologically advanced equipment. Typically, a truck-driver course that lasts five weeks in the U.S. army takes a year for Soviet soldiers from Central Asia. See Murray Feshback, "The Soviet Future: A Different Crisis," *Military Review* 61, no. 6 (June 1981), pp. 34–40, and S. Enders Winbush and Alex Alexiev, *The Ethnic Factor in the Soviet Armed Forces* (Santa Monica, CA: RAND Corp., 1982), Report no. R-2787/1.

68. Amos A. Jordan, "Introduction" in Geoffrey A. Kemp, Robert L. Pfaltzgraff, Jr., and Uri Ra'anan, eds., *The Other Arms Race* (Lexington, MA: D. C. Heath, 1975), p. xlv.

69. James L. Foster, "New Conventional Weapons Technologies: Implications for the Third World," in Ra'anan, Pfaltzgraff, and Kemp, eds., *Arms Transfers to the Third World*, pp. 65–86.

70. Anne Hessing Cahn et al., *Controlling Future Arms Trade* (New York: McGraw-Hill, 1977) p. 89.

71. Capt. J. R. Seesholtz, "Is Technology the Culprit?" *U.S. Naval Institute Proceedings*, June 1982, pp. 46–50. See also S.L.A. Marshall, "Man Against Armor," *Armor*, January–February 1980, pp. 30–31, and his classic, *Men Against Fire* (New York: Random House, 1947), pp. 208–209.

72. James D. James, "Military Cohesion Is an Epoxy That Must Be Mixed Just Right," *Army* 30, no. 11 (November 1980), pp. 7–8, and Deborah Shapley, "The Army's New Fighting Doctrine," *New York Times Magazine*, November 28, 1982, pp. 36–57.

73. Quoted in "Arms and a Continent: Africa's Quest for Power," *New Africa*, August 1981, pp. 16–20. For an earlier, more general discussion of the advantages of such a strategy, see Charles Wolf, Jr., *Some Connections Between Economic and Military Assistance Programs in Underdeveloped Areas* (Santa Monica, CA: RAND Corp., 1961), Report no. P-2389.

74. "The Most African Country: A Survey of Nigeria," *Economist*, January 23, 1982, p. 46. The Nigerian armed forces also have had trouble maintaining Soviet-supplied tanks and keeping track of spare parts generally. See Col. Norman Dodd, "Nigeria's Armed Forces," *Defence Africa*, July–August 1981, pp. 7–10.

Chapter 6

1. A. J. Ventner, *Africa At War* (Greenwich, CT: Devin-Adair, 1974).

2. Gregory Copely, "Africa Begins the Change," *Defense and Foreign Affairs* (October 1979), pp. 6–13.

3. Guy J. Pauker, Steven Canby, A. Ross Johnson, and William B. Quandt, *In Search of Self-Reliance: U.S. Security Assistance to the Third World Under the Nixon Doctrine* (Santa Monica, CA: RAND Corp., 1973), Report no. R-1092-ARPA, p. v.

4. Charles Wolf, Jr., "Economic Success, Stability, and the 'Old' International Order," *International Security* 6, no. 1 (Summer 1981), pp. 75–92. Also see James A. Caporaso, "Industrializing in the Periphery: the Evolving Division of Labor," *International Studies Quarterly* 25, no. 1 (Spring 1981), pp. 347–384.

5. Harry G. Gelber, *Technology, Defense, and External Relations in China, 1975–1978* (Boulder, CO: Westview Press, 1979), p. 87.

6. Stephanie G. Neuman, "Arms Transfers and Economic Development: Some Research and Policy Issues," in Stephanie Neuman and Robert Harkavy, eds., *Arms Transfers in the Modern World* (New York: Praeger, 1979), pp. 219–245.

7. Hans Singer, *Technologies for Basic Needs* (Geneva: International Labour Organisation, 1977), p. 11.

8. E. F. Schumacher, *Small Is Beautiful: Economics As If People Mattered* (New York: Harper and Row, 1973), pp. 145, 176.

9. Charles Weiss, Jr., "Mobilizing Technology for Developing Countries," *Science* 203 (March 16, 1979), pp. 1083–1089.

10. International Labour Organisation, *Technologies for Basic Needs* (Geneva: International Labour Organisation, 1980), pp. 85–86.

11. Richard S. Eckaus, *Appropriate Technologies for Developing Countries* (Washington, D.C.: National Academy of Sciences, 1977), pp. 37–38, 65. Also see James Tobin, "Technological Development and Employment," Discussion Paper no. 190 (Institute for Development Studies, University of Nairobi, Kenya, 1974, mimeo).

12. See Jack N. Behrman and Harvey W. Wallender, *Tranfers of Manufacturing Technology Within Multinational Enterprises* (Cambridge, MA: Ballinger, 1976), pp. 49–65 for successful examples; also Roy F. Wiese, "The Structure of Industrial Training in Kenya and the Role of the Directorate of Industrial Training," Discussion Paper no. 248 (Institute for Development Studies, University of Nairobi, Kenya, 1977), and Carlton R. Williams, "Skills Formation in the Kenyan Informal Economy," Working Paper no. 362 (Institute for Development Studies, University of Nairobi, Kenya, 1980).

13. I am indebted to this official, who asked not to be identified. He also pointed out that appropriate technology is a hands-on issue and that very often well-conceived projects die a bureaucratic death or are crushed in the public- and private-sector rivalry to control development resources. The production orientation of appropriate technology does not permit much process modification, and the projects often create excess capacity because they experience high fixed costs, cannot be used in variable ways, and cannot compete in the export market.

14. T. L. Maliyamkono and Stuart Wells, "Effects of Overseas Training on Economic Development: Impact Surveys on Overseas Training," in T. L. Maliyamkono, ed., *Policy Developments in Overseas Training* (Nairobi: East African Universities Research Project, 1980), pp. 1–37. For comparison, see Wilbert Stitt, Jr., "The African Officer and the Command and General Staff College Experience"

(paper read at the annual meetings of the African Studies Association, San Francisco, CA, 1975, mimeo).

15. See U.S. Congress, House of Representatives, Committee on Foreign Affairs, *Military Assistance Training* (Washington, D.C.: U.S. Government Printing Office, 1970), p. 62. My own experience in three military schools with African officers convinces me that this fear, together with the belief that International Military Education and Training (IMET) program students leave the United States indoctrinated with American culture and political beliefs, is greatly misplaced. Many of the officers I met from Ghana, Zaire, Nigeria, Somalia, Kenya, and Senegal were true professionals, interested in learning as much as they could about the United States and its military, although some were obviously attending the schools as a political reward or vacation. The former did not become automatic supporters of America, because the training they received was most often inappropriate (specific technical skills aside): High ranking officers were enrolled in courses with junior Americans; topics were taught in culturally inappropriate or insensitive ways; few attempts were made to exchange ideas— the presumption was that they were in the United States to learn from us. But most important was the issue of scale. Although the Africans were impressed with U.S. equipment, they were also intimidated by it. U.S. captains regularly could call on (and planned and trained for) more firepower than that of many African armies in toto. These infrastructural assumptions precluded the training being relevant and thus made it boring. The "shopping lists" so feared by U.S. congressmen rarely included arms—more often they included scarce consumer goods, freely available in the post exchange, that would have been unavailable or prohibitively expensive in their home countries.

16. U.S. Congress, Senate, Committee on Foreign Relations, *The Conventional Arms Policy of the United States* (Washington, D.C.: U.S. Government Printing Office, 1980), p. 6.

17. "The Sky's the Limit," *World Business Weekly*, July 27, 1981, pp. 27–39.

18. William S. Lind, "Simple Tanks Would Suffice," *Harpers*, September 1982, pp. 22–24, and "Aren't Four Tanks Better Than One?" *New York Times*, December 1, 1982, p. 30.

19. Fredrick S. Pearson, "U.S. Arms Transfers: The Feasibility of Restraint," *Arms Control* 2, no. 1 (May 1981), pp. 25–49. See also U.S. Congress, House of Representatives, Committee on International Relations, *United States Arms Policies in the Persian Gulf and Red Sea Areas: Past, Present, and Future* (Washington, D.C.: U.S. Government Printing Office, 1977), pp. 174–175.

20. U.S. Congress, *United States Arms Policies in the Persian Gulf and Red Sea Areas*, p. 46.

21. Pamela G. Hollie, "Here Comes Tom Jones Again," *New York Times*, August 2, 1981, p. F1. Incidentally, nearly 1,200 T38s were also built by Northrop.

22. U.S. Congress, House of Representatives, Committee on International Relations, *Conventional Arms Transfer Policy: Background Information* (Washington, D.C.: U.S. Government Printing Office, 1978), pp. 63–64, and Government Accounting Office, *Defense Department Is Not Doing Enough To Maximize Competition When Awarding Contracts For Foreign Military Sales Programs* (Washington, D.C.: U.S. Government Printing Office, 1978), Report no. PSAD 78-147.

23. U.S. Congress, House of Representatives, Committee on Foreign Affairs, *U.S. Security Assistance and Arms Transfer Policies for the 1980s*, pp. 6–7, and *Changing Perspectives on U.S. Arms Transfer Policy*, pp. 26–28, (both are Washington, D.C.: U.S. Government Printing Office, 1981).

24. Chuck Doe, "Foreign Customers Want Best Planes," *Army Times*, December 27, 1982, pp. 14–15. The U.S. Air Force decision not to buy the aircraft has a critical impact regarding logistical support. As soon as the air force, navy, and marines each acquired several F5s as aggressor aircraft (because of its similarity to the MIG21), the logistics of spare parts and maintenance support for foreign F5s became much more efficient because they were "in the system." For examples of the negative effects of such support, see Government Acounting Office, *Foreign Military Sales—A Potential Drain on U.S. Defense Posture* (Washington, D.C.: U.S. Government Printing Office, 1977), Report no. LCD-77-440.

25. Judith Miller, "The Hardware Store Is Open and Customers Come Running," *New York Times*, June 21, 1981, p. E1.

26. Jacques S. Gansler, *The Defense Industry* (Cambridge: MIT Press, 1980), p. 120.

27. AIMVAL/ACEVAL stands for a series of tests evaluating Air Interceptor Missiles and ace pilot combat performance. For discussions of AIMVAL/ACEVAL, see Thomas H. Etzold, *Defense or Delusion? America's Military in the 1980s* (New York: Harper and Row, 1982), pp. 103–104, and Gen. T. R. Milton (USAF, Retired), "The Danger of False Economies," *Air Force Magazine*, August 1982, p. 73.

28. I am indebted to W. E. Baker and Chuck Monroe of Lockheed Corporation for providing me this information.

29. "Guns vs. Butter," *Business Week*, November 29, 1982, pp. 68–76, and William J. Perry and Cynthia A. Roberts, "Winning Through Sophistication: How To Meet the Soviet Military Challenge," *Technology Review*, July 1982, pp. 27–35.

30. Gen. Sir John Hackett, *The Third World War: The Untold Story* (New York: Macmillan, 1982), p. 60; Jeffrey Record, "The Fortunes of War," *Harpers*, April 1980, pp. 19–22; John J. Fialka, "Study Doubts Efficiency of Complex Arms," *Washington Star*, January 31, 1981; Michael R. Gordon, "But Will They Work?" *National Journal* 14, no. 30 (July 24, 1982), pp. 1284–1291; Lt. Col. Dino Lorenzini and Maj. Chuck Fox, "How Much Is Not Enough: The Non-Nuclear Air Battle in NATO's Central Region," *Naval War College Review*, March–April 1980, pp. 58–78.

31. Charles Mohr, "New Wars Show the Power of Military Basics," *New York Times*, June 18, 1982, p. A1; James F. Dunnigan, "New Weapons, Old Truths," *Forbes*, June 21, 1982, pp. 34–35; "Weapons: Which Ones Work," *Economist*, May 29, 1982, p. 20; Clayton Fritchey, "Weapons Spending Won't Substitute for More Soldiers," *Long Island Newsday*, July 19, 1982, p. 8; and a special section of *Washington Quarterly* 5, no. 4 (Autumn 1982), pp. 17–51, featuring essays by Edward N. Luttwak ("On the Meaning of Victory"), Michael Moodie ("Six Months of Conflict"), W. Seth Carns ("The Bekaa Valley Campaign"), and Jeffrey Record ("The Falklands War"). Similar lessons had been learned and

subsequently forgotten in Vietnam and the Yom Kippur War. See Paddy Griffith, *Forward Into Battle: Fighting Tactics from Waterloo to Vietnam* (Sussex, England: Anthony Bird Publications, 1981), pp. 134–135, and Uri Ra'anan, "The New Technologies and the Middle East: 'Lessons' of the Yom Kippur War and Anticipated Developments," in Geoffrey A. Kemp, Robert L. Pfaltzgraff, Jr., and Uri Ra'anan, eds., *The Other Arms Race* (Lexington, MA: D. C. Heath, 1975), pp. 79–90.

32. Michael Moodie, "Sovereignty, Security and Arms," *Washington Papers* 7, no. 67 (1979), p. 24.

33. *Wall Street Journal*, March 19, 1981, p. 31.

34. "Brazil and Cuba Court Africa," *South*, November 1980, pp. 15–18.

35. Government Accounting Office, *Military Sales—An Increasing U.S. Role in Africa* (Washington D.C.: U.S. Government Printing Office, 1978), Report no. ID-77-61, pp. 3–5.

36. See discussion in Chapter 4 on political economy and Baldev Raj Nayar, "Political Mainsprings of Economic Planning in the New Nations," *Comparative Politics* 6, no. 3 (Fall 1974), pp. 341–366.

37. See D.C.R. Heyhoe, *The Alliance and Europe: Part VI, The European Programme*, Adelphi Papers no. 129 (London: International Institute for Strategic Studies, 1980), pp. 2–3, for further definition of these terms. On African airlines, see Jacques Gautrand, "Africa's Expanding Air Network," *World Press Review*, February 1983, p. 54, and "Aviation School Opening," *Daily Nation* (Nairobi), August 26, 1981, p. 3.

38. Doug Richardson, "Upgrading Yesterday's Main Battle Tank," *Defence Africa*, July–August 1981, pp. 15–16, and Simon Durwen, "Armoured Fighting Vehicles for Africa," *Defence Africa*, July–August 1981, pp. 11–12.

Chapter 7

1. Arnold Rivkin, "Arms for Africa?" *Foreign Affairs* 38, no. 1 (October 1959), pp. 84–94. Also see John G. Korman, "United States Military Assistance to Africa: Organization, Problems, and Prospects," Monograph ser. (Carlisle, PA: U.S. Army War College, 1973).

2. David J. Louscher, "U.S. Security Assistance: A Comparative Assessment of Regional Recipients" (paper read at the annual meetings of the International Studies Association, Mexico City, April 1983), p. 10.

3. Harry J. Shaw, "U.S. Security Assistance: Debts and Dependency," *Foreign Policy*, no. 50 (Spring 1983), pp. 105–123.

4. George Gallup, "Americans Disapprove of Arming Other Nations," *Dallas Morning News*, July 23, 1981, p. 50.

5. "The President Got It Wrong About U.S. Aid," *South*, December 1981, pp. 77–78, and Charles Wolf, Jr., *Military Assistance Programs* (Santa Monica, CA: RAND Corporation, 1965), Report no. P-3240. For an excellent, detailed analysis of U.S. assistance to Africa, see Raymond W. Copson, "Africa: Foreign Aid Issues in 1983" (Congressional Research Service, Washington, D.C., March 1983, mimeo). In addition, there are a number of recent U.S. State Department

documents available, including *Security and Economic Assistance for FY 1984,* Current Policy no. 454; *Economics and Politics: The Quandary of Foreign Aid,* Current Policy no. 461; *Our Development Dialog With Africa,* Current Policy no. 462; and *International Security and Development Cooperation Program,* Special Report no. 108 (all are Washington, D.C.: U.S. Government Printing Office, 1983). As this manuscript went to the publisher, the House again reduced the African Security Assistance budget for fiscal year 1984, because, as Rep. Howard Wolpe stated, "the region's economic stagnation cannot be cured by larger and larger military expenditures." Reported in Lexie Verdon, "Arms Aid to African Nations Is Trimmed by House Panel," *Washington Post,* April 14, 1983.

6. Michael R. Gordon, "Competition With the Soviet Union Drives Reagan's Arms Sales Policy," *National Journal,* May 16, 1981, pp. 868–873.

7. U.S. Congress, House of Representatives, Committee on International Relations, *United States Arms Transfer and Security Assistance Programs* (Washington, D.C.: U.S. Government Printing Office, 1978), p. 71.

8. *The Management of Security Assistance* (Wright-Patterson AFB, Ohio: Defense Institute for Security Assistance Management, 1980).

9. Paul Y. Hammond, David J. Louscher, and Michael D. Salomon, "Controlling U.S. Arms Transfers: The Emerging System," *Orbis* 23, no. 2 (Summer 1979), pp. 317–352. See also "Growing Dilemmas for the Management of Arms Sales," *Armed Forces and Society* 5, no. 5 (Fall 1979), pp. 1–20.

10. Richard M. Moose, "Africa: Security Assistance to the Sub-Sahara," *Department of State Bulletin* 78, no. 2013 (April 1978), pp. 30–31.

11. General Accounting Office, *Military Sales—An Increasing U.S. Role in Africa* (Washington, D.C.: U.S. Government Printing Office, 1978), Report no. ID-77-61. Also see a related study by the General Accounting Office, *The Roles and Functions of Overseas Security Assistance Officers Need To Be Clarified* (Washington, D.C.: U.S. Government Printing Office, 1981), Report no. ID 81-47.

12. Robert J. Pranger and Dale R. Tahtinen, *Toward a Realistic Military Assistance Program* (Washington, D.C.: American Enterprise Institute, 1974).

13. "Arms Sales Turn into Gifts for Struggling Third World Nations," *Business Week,* July 25, 1983, p. 5.

14. Phillip J. Farley, Stephen S. Kaplan, and William H. Lewis, *Arms Across the Sea* (Washington, D.C.: Brookings Institution, 1978), p. 38.

15. Stephen Peter Rosen, "Brown Soldiers, White Officers," *Washington Quarterly* 5, no. 2 (Spring 1982), pp. 117–130.

16. Stephanie Neuman, "Security, Military Expenditures, and Socioeconomic Development," *Orbis* 22, no. 3 (Fall 1978), pp. 569–594.

17. Michael D. Masettig, "Military Sales: More Cooperation But a Lot More Competition," *Europe,* May–June 1980, pp. 23–26.

18. Andrew J. Pierre, "Arms Sales: The New Diplomacy," *Foreign Affairs* 60, no. 2 (Winter 1981–82), pp. 266–286.

Abbreviations

AIMVAL/ACEVAL	Air Interceptor Missile and air combat expert performance evaluations
AISSA	Annual Integrated Summary of Security Assistance
CIA	Central Intelligence Agency
DISAM	Defense Institute for Security Assistance Management
FX	fighter export
FMS	Foreign Military Sales
GDP	gross domestic product
GNP	gross national product
IMF	International Monetary Fund
IMET	International Military Education and Training
ILO	International Labour Organization
MAP	Military Assistance Program
MTT	mobile training team
NCW	new conventional weapons
NATO	North Atlantic Treaty Organization
NIC	Newly Industrialized Countries
OAU	Organization of African Unity

Polisario	Popular Front for the Liberation of Saguia el Hamra and Rio de Oro
PGMs	precision-guided munitions
SAM	Surface to Air Missiles
UN	United Nations
UNITA	Union for Total Independence of Angola

Index

Navy," *Defence Africa* (September–October 1981), pp. 3–7; and Mike Gable, "Africa's Navies Are Defining Their Functions, Capabilities, and Budgets," *Defense and Foreign Affairs* (January/February 1982), pp. 13–14, 30–31.

33. Roy Braybrook, "African Air Forces Today," *Defence Africa*, November–December 1980, pp. 5–7, and Bill Gunston, "Combat Aircraft for Africa," *Defence Africa*, November–December 1981, pp. 22–23.

34. Gen. Olusegun Obasanjo, *My Command: An Account of the Nigerian Civil War 1967–1970* (Ibadan: Heinemann, 1980), pp. 84–85.

Chapter 3

1. Joseph P. Smaldone, *Warfare in the Sokoto Caliphate: Historical and Sociological Perspectives* (Cambridge: Cambridge Univesity Press, 1977), p. 94. Also see Jack Goody, *Technology, Tradition, and the State in Africa* (London: Hutchinson, 1971), pp. 39–56.

2. Carlo M. Cipolla, *Guns, Sails, and Empires: Technological Innovation and the Early Phases of European Expansion* (New York: Crowell, 1965).

3. H. J. Fisher and V. Rowland, "Firearms in the Central Sudan," *Journal of African History* 12, no. 2 (1971), pp. 215–239, cited in Smaldone, *Warfare in the Sokoto Caliphate*, pp. 93–94.

4. John Ellis, *The Social History of the Machine Gun* (New York: Pantheon, 1975), p. 95.

5. William P. Avery and Louis A. Picard, "Pull Factors in the Transfer of Conventional Armaments to Africa," *Journal of Political and Military Sociology* 8, no. 1 (Spring 1980), pp. 55–70.

6. "Divisions in Diplomacy," *Time*, March 1, 1982, pp. 12–14.

7. Luther J. Carter, "Global 2000 Report: Vision of a Gloomy World," *Science* 209 (August 1, 1980), pp. 575–576, and U.S. Arms Control and Disarmament Agency (hereafter cited as USACDA), *World Military Expenditures and Arms Transfers, 1970–1979* (Washington, D.C.: U.S. Government Printing Office, 1982).

8. John Stanley and Maurice Rearton, *The International Trade in Arms* (New York: Praeger, 1972), p. 81. Also see Basil Collier, *Arms and the Men: The Arms Trade and Governments* (London: Hamish Hamilton, 1980); Russell Warren Howe, *Weapons: The International Game of Arms, Money, and Diplomacy* (Garden City, NY: Doubleday, 1980); and Cynthia A. Cannizzo, ed., *The Gun Merchants: Politics and Policies of the Major Arms Suppliers* (New York: Pergamon, 1980).

9. Andrew J. Pierre, "Arms Sales: The New Diplomacy," *Foreign Affairs* 60, no. 2 (Winter 1981–82), pp. 266–286. See also his recent book, *The Global Politics of Arms Sales* (Princeton: Princeton University Press, 1982).

10. Robert E. Harkavy, *The Arms Trade and International Systems* (Cambridge: Ballinger, 1975), p. 14.

11. Maj. Gen. K. Perkins, "Winning Friends: A Military Strategy in the Third World," *Royal United Services Institute*, June 1981, pp. 39–41.

12. See, for example, Mary Kaldor, *The Baroque Arsenal* (New York: Hill and Wang, 1981).

13. USACDA, *World Military Expenditures*, pp. 3–8.

14. See Bruce J. Palmer, Jr., "U.S. Security Interests and Africa South of the Sahara," *AEI Defense Review* 2, no. 6 (1978), entire issue; William H. Lewis, "How a Defense Planner Looks at Africa," in Helen Kitchen, ed., *Africa: From Mystery to Maze* (Washington, D.C.: The Third Century Corporation, 1978), pp. 277–304; Richard Sales, "The Core of Modern Conflict," *Defense and Foreign Affairs* (June 1981), pp. 20–21; James Ridgeway, "Strategic Minerals Down Under," *Defense Week*, August 3, 1981, p. 5; and U.S. Congress, House of Representatives, Committee on Foreign Affairs, *The Possibility of a Resource War in Southern Africa* (Washington, D.C.: U.S. Government Printing Office, 1981).

15. Quoted in Leopold Sedar Senghor, "Africa and America," in Michael A. Samuels, ed., *Africa and the West* (Boulder, CO: Westview Press, 1980), pp. 12–25.

16. USACDA, *World Military Expenditures.*

17. This summary is based in part on that in the introduction to Andrew J. Pierre, ed., *Arms Transfers and American Foreign Policy* (New York: New York University Press, 1979), pp. 4–5. See also the introduction to Bruce E. Arlinghaus, ed., *Arms for Africa* (Lexington, MA: D. C. Heath, 1983).

18. See Dale R. Tahtinen, *Arms in the Indian Ocean: Interests and Challenges* (Washington, D.C.: American Enterprise Institute, 1977); U.S. Congress, House of Representatives, Committee on International Relations, *United States Arms Policies in the Persian Gulf and Red Sea Areas: Past, Present, and Future* (Washington, D.C.: U.S. Government Printing Office, 1977); "U.S., Somalia Move Toward Pact on Access to Military Facilities," *Washington Post*, August 12, 1980; "Arms in the Ocean," *South*, November 1980, pp. 19–20; George C. Wilson, "Panel Cool to Selling Arms to Somalia in Exchange for the Right to Use Ports," *Washington Post*, August 27, 1980; Charles T. Bowers, "Berbera—It's U.S. Turn at Strategic Site," *Los Angeles Times*, September 6, 1980; and "The Horn of Africa Trumpets War," *Economist*, March 6, 1982, pp. 59–60.

19. Kathleen Teltsch, "Reporter's Notebook: New Flag and Old Wars at the U.N.," *New York Times*, September 21, 1979, p. A2.

20. Edgar O'Ballance, *No Victor, No Vanquished: The Yom Kippur War* (London: Presidio Press, 1978); and Robert E. Harkavy, "Arms Resupply *During* Conflict: A Framework for Analysis" (paper presented at the Georgetown University Center for Strategic and International Studies, Washington, D.C., November 1981). Dr. Harkavy is currently engaged in a long-term research project on the subject at the U.S. Army War College, Carlisle Barracks, PA, and will be publishing a book based upon his research in the near future.

21. Ariel Levite and Athanassios Platias, "Arms Transfers and Leverage" (paper presented at the annual meetings of the International Studies Association, Cincinnati, OH, March 1982). See also S. D. Muni, *Arms Buildup and Development: Linkages in the Third World*, Canberra Papers on Strategy and Defence no. 22 (Canberra: Australian National University Press, 1981), and Jay Ross, "Mugabe Rejects U.S. Linkage of Issues," *Washington Post*, May 27, 1981.

22. U.S. Army War College, *Effectiveness of U.S. Security Assistance in Acquiring and Retaining Friends and Allies*, Publication no. ACN 79016 (Carlisle Barracks, PA: Strategic Studies Institute, 1980).